Hoosier

Hauntings

Thunder Bay Press

Hoosier
Hauntings

K.T. MacRorie

Thunder Bay Press

Published by Thunder Bay Press
Designed and typeset by Maureen MacLaughlin-Morris
Publisher: Sam Speigel
Cover design by Lynda A. Bass
Cover layout by Adventures with Nature, East Lansing, MI
Illustrations by Patrick Reed
Photographs by Author
Printed by Dickinson Press, Grand Rapids, MI

ISBN: 1-882376-37-4

Printed in the United States of America

97 98 99 2000   1 2 3 4 5 6 7 8 9

Other titles in the Thunder Bay *Tales of the Supernatural* series:

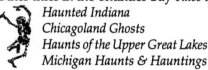

Haunted Indiana
Chicagoland Ghosts
Haunts of the Upper Great Lakes
Michigan Haunts & Hauntings

THANKS & KUDOS

I would like to express my most heartfelt thanks to all who have shared their stories and have helped over the past four years to bring this project to fruition. There are far too many to name individually, but among them are,

Barbara Carney, Vesper Cook, Keith Corman, Tony Cotten, Stacey and Julie Doose, Frederick P. Griffin, Carol Haas, J. Hartman, Lee Holloway, William Hower, Libbe Hughes, Saundra Jessee, Maxine Kruse, Reann Lydick, Tina Mellot, Mary Renshaw, S. Reznik, Mark and Kathy Spaeth, Phyllis Walters, R.B. Wetherill, M.D., Shirley Willard, and Chris Woodyard.

Also my thanks to these wonderful institutions who donated research time and materials to this project:

The Cincinnati Recreation Commission, Clark Co. Library, The Culbertson Mansion State Historic Site, Elkhart Co. Historical Museum, Fulton Co. Historical Society, Hendricks Co. Historical Society, Kestrel Publications, Lawrence Co. Tourism Commission, Miami Co. Historical Society, Monroe Co. Historical Society, Northern Indiana Historical Society, Plainfield Public Library, Vigo Co. Historical Society and the Willard Library.

To

My father

and to all who keep alive the
great tradition of the story teller,
this book is fondly dedicated.

TABLE OF CONTENTS

INDIANA
Where The Dead Still Wander...

I would like to point out that, contrary no doubt to the reader's esteemed opinion, I am definitively, totally and without a doubt a skeptic when it comes to the realm of the unseen. I am not unduly terrified by the prospect of a ghost hanging around some musty bedroom. On the other hand, I do not go poking around damp unlit basements, go prowling over back country roads at two in the morning searching for strange patches of fog, or deliberately seek out, just for the purposes of scaring the bejesus out of myself, haunted sites. I have no particular desire, under most circumstances, to see a ghost as I turn the corner of a hallway in some dark, under-lit Victorian nightmare of a home.

When I say that I am a skeptic, what I mean is that for ninety-nine percent of the "haunted sites" that I have visited or researched, I have found rational, reasonable everyday answers to the questions of what goes bump in the night. I believe that many haunted places are a product of urban myth and a precise set of environmental conditions which are usually explainable. This is not to say, however, that I have never seen a ghost. It's simply an experience I do not deliberately strive to attain.

I have lived around, played upon, and worked in haunted places for as long as I can remember. When I was a child, my family would venture out to visit relatives of my father. These relatives, who lived quite a piece from our home, owned a century-and-a-half old three-story farm house which jutted out on a finger of land in the middle of a wonderfully placid lake. Yet the house was anything but placid. A lot of living—and a lot of dying for that matter—had gone on in that house, which has always been owned by the same family. And over the years, many people experienced strange occurrences they could not explain. Lights floating down hallways, the soft patter of a child's feet lightly treading down the stairs, a presence watching over a beloved grand piano. I was both terrified and fascinated by that house, and although I haven't visited my relatives for quite a few years now, I'm sure that whatever shares their house continues to make its daily, or nightly, rounds.

As a high school student involved with community theater back in my home town of Cincinnati, Ohio, I had the opportunity to work with, and see, my first ghost. Wesley, the disembodied caretaker of the theater where our group performed, would every night make sure the doors were locked and all persons were out of the building, going so far as to peer at both my best friend and I as we talked in the parking lot one evening after locking up the building, just to make sure we weren't up to any mischief. Wesley watched us for about ten minutes through a basement window, the drapes pulled aside by his right hand, until he turned away, leaving the curtains to fall back in place.

These run-ins with the unseen were not something I desired to have happen. And generally, they were experiences that I kept to myself. Believe me, you get mighty strange looks from people when it comes to discussing the dearly departed. Yet frightening as these intersections with the unseen are, I can't help but be fascinated, as I am sure many of you are, as to why these souls continued to walk, float, or stand among the living.

But what exactly is a ghost? Science can't quiet prove their existence. Our reason denies their reality. And our faith refuses to accept their possibility. Yet they are there, unseen and unfelt, until the right moment, the right person, the right opportunity comes along, and WHAM, there they are; a cold spot in the middle of a room, a breeze in an airtight hallway, voices and sounds from dead space, or misty images of those who have gone before us. They reach out to us, some pleading, some angry and desperate, striving to talk, to tell us their desperate bits of information, to hear once again the warmth of a human voice in that realm where there is no warmth. But why? What brings them back time after time to plead their unknown cause; they, trapped in their unknown world; we, in this mortal coil?

Many researchers have theorized that trauma or sudden death can lead to a haunting. A person, taken quickly and unexpectedly from life, may not realize consciously what has happened. They latch on mentally or psychically, to what they recognize, what is familiar, and there they remain until they come to an understanding of their new situation.

Others believe that buildings themselves can pick up, like a tape recorder, the resonances of life. Science has recently shown us that we all, young and old, emit an electromagnet field, a charge of energy. This field, or aura, has even been photographed reliably by Kirlian photography, a technique which registers the electromagnetic discharges of living beings. Just as a battery stores energy, which under correct circumstances is released as electricity, so too perhaps a house, an electrical field all its own, can store, like some great capacitor, the discharges from living, the resonances of our own electromagnetic fields. And just as batteries need the right environment to work their magic, these vaults of energy likewise need the correct setting, the right receptors, such as people who have learned to be attuned to these discharges. You can hook a battery up to a chunk of wood, and nothing happens. But put them in a flashlight, and presto, a visible response. Add water, and the results can be truly electrifying.

Water seems to have an interesting link to the paranormal. Many haunted sites, be they houses, fields, or roads, are located near bodies of water. Underground springs or water tables, streams or creeks, lakes and so forth may play a part in how well electromagnetic energy is discharged, stored, and eventually transferred to a sensitive person.

In Irish folklore, all one needed to do to escape from the denizens of the Unseelie Court, the nasty wights that inhabited the hills and fens of the countryside, was to cross a moving body of fresh water, such as a stream or river. Once on the other side, the pursued was out of harm's way. Washington Irving, author of *The Legend of Sleepy Hollow*, even worked that theory into his classic tale. If poor Ichabod Crane managed to cross the bridge over the river, then the headless horseman could not pursue him any further. Perhaps these people were on to something. Maybe they realized the relationship between water and the paranormal and translated it into their folklore and legends. But perhaps there is no safety zone, that no matter how far we run, we can never outdistance that which scares us the most, the threat of the unseen.

Indiana has long had many tales of the unnatural and unexplained floating about its many counties and cities. Ghosts were such a problem back in 1903 that a front page article about the haunting of houses in Indianapolis and the distress they had caused rental agents was published. One house had six renters in three months because a stubborn spirit would run tirelessly up and down the stairway all night long, making enough noise to keep everyone awake, but never appearing before the tenant. Other houses where murders had taken place would be vacated when tenants complained of dripping blood or mysterious screams at the exact hour of the grisly death.

I have attempted to research each site through visits, personal accounts, interviews with those who experienced the unexplained, and photos where possible. I do not claim to be psychic. I don't read tarot cards, attend seances or see auras. Like I said, I'm a skeptic. I look for reason to explain the mysterious. But there are always those few places that reason can not explain away. I believe that where science fails, the intuition must take over.

Who really knows what roams the fields and homes of Indiana, waiting for a receptive person to come along, to step into their sphere of influence. To the skeptical, all I can say is keep an open mind. Who knows, one day you may need it to deal with the impossible. To the rest, relax. That noise you just heard—nothing more than the foundation settling. That moan—just the furnace coming on. The rattle of the door— just the wind catching at the hinges. After all, if, as our license plates have claimed all along, things both seen and unseen "Wander Indiana," then perhaps it's nothing more than the dead coming "Home Again."

Note: A name with an asterisk means that the name was changed either at the request of the person involved, or because I couldn't find the person and ask permission to use their real name. If you are one of these persons and are surprised to see your story here, please contact me.

CHAPTER ONE

WHAT IS A GHOST?
A Spectral Definition

Before we dive into the darkness lurking behind the amber waves of grain of the Indiana landscape, we might want to try to better understand what it is that we are seeing when that misty apparition comes floating down the stairs in the dead of night towards us.

The word "apparition" comes from Latin, and literally means "to appear." According to the 1993 Encyclopedia of Psychic Phenomena, there are two basic forms of apparitions: those which are spontaneous, and those which are induced. The spontaneous we are familiar with, and will be seeing many examples of within these pages. I tend to shy away from the "induced" phenomena, either in dubious skepticism targeted towards those who for sensationalistic reasons claim to be able to summon up an apparition, or in true worry and fear over those haunted sites that have inadvertently been negatively magnified somehow by either seemingly innocent or at times decidedly deliberate occult practices.

But what is a ghost? Ebenezer Scrooge dismissed his first phantom visitor as a "bit of undigested cheese." But a ghost is more than the result of a late night snack, unless perhaps that snack is Taco Bell. You might loosely define a ghost as a visual apparition of a deceased human being, or in some cases, of a deceased animal. A ghost is also many times the image or phantom of a specific person directly related to the time or place it appears. This is different from a haunting.

A haunting, more generally, is considered to be a place or locality said to be visited by unseen forces. These forces can manifest themselves in a variety of ways such as unexplainable noises, strange or out-of-place smells, spots or drafts of extreme cold, displacement or complete disappearance of objects, visual images, tactile sensations, disembodied voices or psychokinetic movement of objects. This is not to say that a ghost cannot appear in the same locale as a haunting. As a matter of fact, that is many times the case. But the two are not inextricably linked.

The paranormal force that is the most unnerving is the visual apparition, the image of a loved one, or of a prior inhabitant of our home. Sometimes comforting, many times frightening, always startling, these are the apparitions we all fear "go bump in the night." Paranormal researchers who study visual apparitions through both accepted and non-conventional scientific methods have grouped these ghosts into seven roughly-defined categories.

Crisis apparitions make up the first group. These are ghostly encounters with the deceased who return at a time of crisis to try to intervene. We have all heard of tales of the much-loved husband or wife returning from beyond to inform their spouse of the location of a previously unknown insurance policy, just when the family is bordering on financial ruin.

The second group, perhaps the most common, is simple apparitions of the dead. Seeing a former inhabitant of a building, a ghostly employee still doing their job, or any disincarnate being still roaming the physical world. Many times these ghosts appear as a replaying movie, always caught up in the same act. The phantom that always wanders the hall at a precise hour or season. The replay of a murder over and over, much to the horror of the viewer. They can just as easily be associated with a particular place or family as not, and seem to care not, at least most of the time, about us and our activities.

Collective apparitions are intriguing, to say the least. This third group of rare phenomena almost seem like religious experiences in retrospect. These sightings are apparitions of the dead that occur simultaneously to multiple witnesses in different places. A woman in Indianapolis might see the ghost of her father, while at the same instant, her mother in South Bend sees her beloved husband.

The fourth group, reciprocal apparitions, go beyond ghosts and into the realm of quantum physics. In these cases, two people see each other simultaneously through some anomaly in time. Each person appears as a ghost to the other, and both are equally surprised by the event. In a reciprocal apparition, you, as the viewer, might perceive a gentleman, dressed in antique garb, going about his business, who then glances up, and with an astonished look on his face, sees you as well. Both you and he are puzzled, as you both are "out of place" to the eyes of the other. These apparitions usually are short-lived, and if you but glance away, the vision vanishes.

The type of apparition that researchers constantly crave are veridical apparitions. These are sightings that can be corroborated through scientific or physical documentation, such as photographs, sound recordings, video tapes, or other scientific methods. EVP, or electronic voice phenomena, while not exactly a ghost, falls into this category.

EVP has gained much recognition in the past few years as one of the newest, and most strange paranormal occurrences. In an EVP occurrence, sensitive listening and recording devices are placed in appropriate places, such as mausoleums or greatly disturbed sites. A constant recording is made during an entire night, and many times, as the tape is analyzed, strange, fragmented voices can be heard very faintly on the tape, as if from speaking from a far-off place. Every precaution is taken to ensure that there is no chance for tampering or interference from any outside source. Yet the voices are there. Science still has no explanation.

The sixth group, deathbed apparitions, are the type we all hope to experience during our last moments on this earth, when a loved one appears to comfort us and lead us on into the light of the next existence. These types of encounters are most often reported by individuals who have gone through near-death experiences.

Reincarnate apparitions are most common to Native American groups and practitioners of their Native American religions. In these cases, a recently deceased loved one reappears to a family member in the guise of its next reincarnation, to identify themselves both to the family they have left, and to the family they will soon join as a reincarnate being.

Finally, there is an elusive eighth group that may or may not be classified as apparitions; those of the poltergeist. Poltergeist is the combination of two German words: poltern, meaning "to knock," and Geist, meaning "spirit." Together, you might consider poltergeist to mean "noisy spirit." Traditionally a particularly pesky type of apparition that haunted many a home, recent research has hinted that poltergeist phenomena may actually be linked to psychokinetic energy randomly released by an adolescent youth. In the bulk of poltergeist cases, the afflicted family is composed of two parents and at least one adolescent child, many times a young girl. Researchers and psychologists have suggested that perhaps manifesting poltergeist activity is a way for the adolescent to express hostility without the fear of punishment or retribution. Poltergeist activity is also generally short-lived, ranging anywhere from a few days to six months. It usually quickly starts, and just as quickly ceases. For these reasons, and others, I have not explored poltergeists in the following pages.

Now that we know what to call a ghost when we run into—or through—one, what causes them? Are they the guilt-ridden conscience of the deceased, unable to move into the next life before making amends for their wrongs? Are they the violently killed, who could not, at the time of their death, grasp the fact that they were indeed dead? Some have suggested that ghosts are hallucinations, products of the imagination brought into play by overactive minds. Yet too many ghosts have been seen by rational, unimaginative people over the years.

Some paranormal researchers have theorized that apparitions are an amalgam of personality patterns, manifesting themselves in one generic form, male or female. They use this theory to explain the phantom soldiers that seem to wander Civil War battlefields, single representations of the many who fell.

Eastern religions have long held that thoughts are more than just mental processes, that they have weight and reality. Perhaps ghosts are the projection of the human unconscious mind (called a *tulpa* by Tibetan monks), a thought-form come to life.

Localized phenomena, or the physical location of an area, may play a part in ghostly sightings. Perhaps a Native American burial site or an underground stream can create a flowing energy around a residence. Could it be that all those power lines overhead form a electromagnetic grid inside which other electromagnetic phenomena can reign? There has been some very loose recent research that speculates on the nature of electricity and how it effects our lives.

There is a final theory of which I am rather fond that a chemist friend of mine developed. He uses known and proven chemical and electrical principles to explain the varied phenomena encountered at many haunted sites. He theorizes that the physical act of living, or being alive and being human, generates and radiates electrochemical, or perhaps, electromagnetic radiation. This possibility has been hinted at through such phenomena as auras and Kirlian photography, where a halo of light, varying in color, seems to surround all living things, even plants. This nonlethal radiation, he reasons, is very strong and takes centuries to dissipate. For example, a three-thousand-year old mummy from ancient Egypt subjected to Kirlian photography still radiates a very weak energy field thousands of years after it was placed in the sarcophagus.

Perhaps physical matter, just as it is affected by normal radiation, is also affected by this living energy. This energy imprints itself onto matter, in patterns unique to each person that passes through any given structure. These patterns are then stored by the structure in question, a house for example, for a period of time dependent on many variables, much like a battery. Temperature, humidity, even the structural components of the house itself, may affect how well or how long a given structure can hold this energy, which will slowly dissipate over time.

The final factor to his theory is people. Some people, perhaps due to their specific chemical balance or electromagnetic field, can sense or see these patterns imprinted on a structure. If the house is a battery, then these people are the wiring that enables the house to release its stored energy. This would explain why some people see ghosts at a haunted sight and why some don't.

And just as a battery loses its potency through continued use, maybe haunted sights diminish in strength over time, relative to the strength of charge or the amount of living they have been subjected to in the first place. A structure that has seen centuries of living may be extremely slow to lose its charge, as each sensitive person draws a little "juice" away. But a newer house, maybe, which has only seen, say, sixty years of living, might drain away quicker.

Who knows? Maybe there *is* some electro-magnetic-chemical explanation to ghosts and hauntings that science has yet to discover or understand. It certainly would make things convenient if it all could be dismissed away in scientific terms. But would that be any fun? I don't think so. After all, would you be reading this book right now if you didn't, in some small way, enjoy be scared by the unseen, the untouchable? Maybe there are some things that we, as humans, simply were never meant to know . . .

CHAPTER TWO

BRIDGE ON THE RIVER "CRY"
Cry-baby Bridges
and
Other Unnatural Overpasses

Haunted bridges seem to proliferate in Indiana. There are more stories of bridges with entombed workers or cases of infants being hurled over the sides than any other type of ghost story I have run into in my research. Perhaps the tragedy and horror of being buried alive, imprinted on our collective unconscious, has given birth to these many tales. Perhaps once, somewhere, a woman actually did tragically slip and lose hold of the precious bundle she was carrying. Or perhaps, there is something more mysterious and undefinable about these spans reaching out across the vast chasms of empty air and lost time . . .

The Avon Bridge

Out on County Road 625E, just south of State Road 36, in Washington Township, stands the Avon Bridge. It may look like an ordinary railroad bridge reaching out over a creek and a county road, but stories persist of the structure spanning more than mere physical dimensions.

The 50-foot-high bridge, built of formed concrete in 1907, has three main arches. Surmounting these arches is a second level of smaller arches, which have small passages between them, giving the impression of a forlorn Roman aqueduct. These chambers often sheltered hobos, giving rise to several ghost stories about the spirits roaming the bridge and the surrounding woods. Other tales tell of terrible construction accidents in which workers were buried alive in the wet cement.

Perhaps the most famous story is of a young mother who was carrying her sick infant to the doctor.

Picture the scene almost a century ago. It was dark, late at night. A cold drizzle cuts through the thick air, chilling even more the clinging mist that penetrates everything it touches. Our young woman in this case, tired and sick with worry over the health of her little one, realizes that her child is not getting any better; indeed has taken a severe turn for the worse.

Perhaps the infant's fever had spiked suddenly. Or maybe its heartbeat, thin and frail at best, had begun to falter. We'll never know. But the mother knew. She knew that the life of her precious child was coming perilously close to the end. What mother would not risk death itself to try and save her child? She bundles herself and the infant up as best as she can in their poor clothes, and desperately starts out through the cutting rain. She has to get to town, to the doctor's office. And the only way to accomplish that is to cross the Avon Bridge late at night.

Now if any of you in your wilder moments have ever ventured out on a railroad overpass, you know firsthand that even in broad daylight on a hot summer afternoon, the footing is at best uncertain. Open gaps wide enough to swallow a leg or break an ankle slice down between each tie, and one has to move with extreme caution to reach the other side. Now picture crossing at night in the rain.

The desperate mother, her mind clouded with worry for her child, sets out to cross the bridge, and perhaps she does go carefully and slowly at first. But no more than halfway across, to late to escape, she sees the light and hears the cry of a train whistle. With nowhere else to go, she turns and in a panic tries to run back to the other side to escape the approaching locomotive. But now she is not as careful as she was going out on the span. Her very life depends on speed. And she almost makes it. Just within sight of safety, her foot slips and catches between the rail and the tie, lodging against the protruding edge of a railroad spike. She twists and turns in a desperate jig to free her foot as the train bears down on her, and in the last instant, her shoe breaks free and she lunges to the other side. But as she falls to safety, her precious cargo, the infant that had brought her out on such a night, slips from her grasp and plummets silently over the edge to the hard ground below.

Distraught at the loss of her child, the poor woman never recovers. She dies of shock shortly thereafter. But still, even today, here in the tail end of the twentieth century, if you listen closely in the still of the night, you can still hear the woman's grief-stricken wails for her lost child as she vainly searches for her little one on the bridge that took her life.[1]

Another tale of the strange Avon Bridge, details the grisly death of a worker during its construction. It seems that when the construction of the bridge was in progress, an itinerant railroad carpenter was sawing a board on a scaffolding. Just as concrete was being poured into the footing, he lost his balance and fell into the hardening concrete. Workers tried vainly to rescue him, but the concrete hardened too fast, and he was sealed in for eternity. Or was he? On many a moonlit night, it is said that his screams can be heard piercing the night air when a train rattles overhead disturbing his rest, and some people claim to have seen his saw protruding through the concrete in a vain attempt to cut his way out.[2]

One last tale surfaces about the dreaded Avon Bridge. Apparently, a high-school student stayed too long at the house of his girlfriend. When he noticed the lateness of the hour, he left in a rush and hurried home so as not to get punished too severely. In order to save time, he decided to take a shortcut over the bridge. When he got about halfway across, he heard a train whistle and saw the light of a train coming down the track. In the dark he didn't know exactly where he was in relation to the terrain beneath him, so he decided to risk a jump from the bridge rather than get run over by the speeding locomotive. He jumped, and quickly realized he had jumped into the deepest part of the ravine over which the bridge ran. Realizing that he would perish from the fall, he screamed his last dying breath just before he hit bottom. It is said that you can hear a train whistle and a few seconds later, a scream, from the boy who jumped off the Avon Bridge.

The New Point Bridge

In Greensburg, there are two more bridges that sound mysteriously like the Avon Bridge. Pat Smith, news columnist for the *Greensburg Daily News*, reported that an elderly man, now dead, related to her this chilling story. Years ago, while he was helping to build the railroad bridge at New Point, one of the workers fell into the cement. There would have been too much time lost if the other workers had gone to the trouble of getting the now-dead man out of the cement, so they just left him there, buried. His spirit does not, and will not, rest as long as the bridge remains standing. His ghostly image can be seen on the bridge from time to time. The bridge at Sandusky is also reportedly haunted by another worker killed in the same manner as the New Point Bridge.

The Danville Bridge

Ronald Baker, in his book *Hoosier Folk Legends*, reports of a bridge in Danville. While it was being built one of the workmen fell into the form filling rapidly with wet cement. His workers tried desperately to save him, but to no avail. The railroad company agreed to fish the poor soul's body out, but only if the workers would pay for the extra time and expense. Since they were but poor railroad workers with not a dime to spare, it just wasn't possible.

Construction proceeded on schedule, but the supports from where the unfortunate man fell were reported to shed "tears" of blood for the entombed man. And when it was time to remove the supports from the newly-poured bridge-cum-tomb, the deceased's forearm, complete with crosscut saw still clutched firmly in its hand, was found somehow protruding from the side of the cement pylon. Rather than undo their work and fall behind schedule, the other workmen simply cut the offending appendage away.

On nights during a full moon, the dead workman would prowl the bridge, trying to stop each train that passed, desperate for a ride. And when each in turn would pass by him into the night, chill screams would rise up into the air as the figure resumed his search for his missing arm and saw.[3]

The Mooresville Bridge

In Central Indiana, outside of Mooresville, there stands a concrete bridge that was built many years ago. During construction, one of those pesky slick-footed workers once again fell into the wet cement. By the time the other workers realized what had happened, he was dead. The concrete had become solid, so they didn't bother trying to remove the body. One arm hung out over the edge of the concrete, just dangling there, so the other workers simply cut the arm off and smeared some cement over the stump to blend in the wound with the rest of the work.

It is said that the arm will from time to time appear and point, not at anything particularly special. Although it's rumored that, if you happen to see the arm sticking out of the decaying pylon, and the fingers of the hand point at you in desperate gesture, you might as well make out your will, for you will die within three days of being singled out by the phantom arm.[4]

The Azalia Bridge

Near the town of Azalia, another bridge is haunted by a woman who conceived a child out of wedlock. She was a social outcast of Azalia for many years, and she turned to isolating herself. This woman supposedly went insane and threw her baby off the bridge into the water. Afterwards, wracked with guilt and remorse for her actions, she lurked for many years around the creek bed and the foot of the bridge, draped in heavy black, mourning the death of her child, a death she herself had brought about.

If you go to the Azalia Bridge and look down over the edge, you might see the image of that poor woman's baby, wrapped tightly in a white blanket, lying in the edge waters of the creek, crying for its mother. And sometimes, if you look down the empty expanse of iron and wood track, you can glimpse the image of the desperate mother herself, draped in black, and can hear her weeping.[5]

Purple Head Bridge

Purple Head Bridge

Purple Head Bridge in Vincennes is a decrepit train bridge with most of the ties now missing, leaving holes through its span like the gaps of rotten teeth. One false step would send the explorer straight down to a tumultuous, rocky demise in the river bottom below. The rusted metal frame however still spans the Wabash, an echo of the might of the former rail traffic that connected a nation before the advent of interstates and air commerce.

During the bloody years of the French and Indian War, and in the early days of settlement thereafter in the land that only later came to be called Indiana, skirmishes between white settlers and Native Americans were fought continually along the banks of the Wabash, leaving many dead on both sides. And as is the way with war, many a time the bodies of those fallen would not receive proper burial.

So it went for one particular shaman of one of the local tribes. Killed in one of the early outbreaks of fighting, his body, despite the best efforts of his own people to get it back out of the captured land, did not receive proper burial, and his soul was not properly sent into the next realm. According to local Vincennes lore, if you make your way out across the bridge, a feat brave in and of itself these days, and wait near the center of the precipitous drop, the bloated purple head of the lost Indian shaman will appear before you, luminous and pale, begging and pleading to be properly buried and released from his earthly imprisonment. The shaman's head has been seen by many witnesses over the years, but the color does not always ring true. One enterprising witness who encountered the shaman's head swore that it's actually blue.

The Dublin Bridge

Many years ago, when automobiles were new and there was no such thing as an experienced driver, it is told that a young woman, her infant daughter on her lap, was driving too fast on her way home over the dark and narrow Dublin Bridge, rain making the tenuous surface even more treacherous. Hitting a bad hole, her auto was thrown against the wooden side rail with such an impact that her baby was thrown clear of the vehicle, over the rail, and into the night-black waters of the creek below.

The hysterical woman searched in vain for her precious cargo, but all to no avail. Her daughter was never found. Driven mad from sadness, the woman would wander the bridge and creek valley searching for her lost daughter until she died from malnutrition and grief. But her spirit is still tied to that dark overpass. If you drive across the Dublin Bridge at night, in the rain, she will come running to your car, begging and pleading you to help her in her vain attempt to find that which was long ago lost.

Allegedly, two inquisitive teens attempted to prove the legend true by picking the stormiest night of summer a few years back. They drove slowly over the span, rain splattering against their windshield, their headlights cutting twin swaths into the blackness of night, when a rain soaked figure appeared out of the gloom. She ran at them, begging for help. The two quickly lost their nerve and spun away, the woman's fingernails screeching along their doors as she frantically grasped at her chance to find her daughter.[6]

Are these strange tales true? Some people swear they are. With luck, we'll never find out. It could be that many of these tales were created, just as are many other myths, as warnings to wayward children to stay away from the dangerous overpasses, where death from falls, trains, or desperate hobos were as real a concern as drugs and drunk drivers are to today's parents. Or maybe, just maybe, these eerie specters are waiting for us to take a stroll, out over the gap of unbelievability, to meet us face on, beckoning us to join them in their midnight observances.

CHAPTER THREE

AS COLD AS DEATH
Cemetery Haunts and Unusual Graves

*". . . no event is so terribly well adapted to inspire the
mental and bodily distress as is burial before death. The
unendurable oppression of the lungs, the stifling fumes
from the damp earth, the clinging of the death garments,
the rigid embrace of the narrow house, the blackness of the
absolute night, the silence like a sea that overwhelms . . ."*
Edgar Allen Poe, "The Premature Burial"

What is it about cemeteries that haunts our imagination?
The grave beckons to us, both abhorrent and fascinating. We
know we are destined to lay there, yet we search for understanding of its mysteries to ease our earthly minds as to the
disposition of our souls. We tell ourselves that there is nothing more to these places than stone, nothing more. Yet what
was that wisp of mist that only now just darted behind the
mausoleum, just out of our vision, beckoning us closer, ever
closer . . .

In Memory of a Little Girl

Over the centuries, stories have surfaced of the wandering
carpenter or stone mason, who mysteriously appears in a town,
completes a task, usually for a grieving family or for a group
that desperately needs help, and vanishes as soon as the work
is completed. There's a story that deals with an impossible staircase, and a mysterious carpenter. Apparently, the large circular staircase that was needed in the construction of a new
church was simply impossible to build in the space provided.
It should have been built first, and the church erected around
it. According to the story, a traveling carpenter arrived one

day and offered to solve the problem. The rest of the workers scoffed, but told him that if he wanted to waste his time, go right ahead. The strange man was seen taking some measurements as the rest of the work crew went home for the night.

But when the work crews returned the next morning, the carpenter was gone, and in his place was a beautiful staircase elegantly built into the impossible space. As the workers examined it in awe, a sudden realization was made; each riser of the staircase was supported by the one *above* it! The strange man would have had to build the stairs from the top down! And except for that support, no other means of bracing was used. It was an architectural miracle. Other cases such as this one have been too well documented to simply dismiss as urban myth. Could it be divine intervention in our midst, the work of guardian angels, or perhaps the craftsmanship of the master carpenter himself, St. Joseph? Here is one such case that can not so easily be brushed away.

There is a very unusual stone in the cemetery at Crown Hill in Salem. Passersby have stopped to admire its lines many times over the years. The memorial stone is an intricately-carved statue of a little girl standing at a gate, carved in 1901 by an unknown stonemason in memory of Caddy Naugle. Caddy was the daughter of Salem monument maker, John Naugle and his wife Mary. The story, which has been told around Salem for nearly a century, tells of the undying love of a father for his daughter. According to the tale, the brightest part of the day for little Caddy was swinging on the front gate of her yard late in the afternoon, waiting for her father, John, to come home from his work at his monument studio.

But those happy days came to an abrupt end in 1901 when Caddy unexpectedly sickened and died at the tender age of only four years. Her father was so disturbed by the death of his little girl that his business greatly suffered, stones were left unfinished, orders never begun, and work backed up. But then one day, just as things seemed bleakest, an itinerant mason appeared asking for a job.

Something about the man made a deep impression on John, and the man was hired at once. Much to John's approval, the wanderer proved to be an excellent mason, but as soon as he had heard of the tragic death of his employer's little girl, he felt deeply that he wanted to help the Naugles to somehow ease their suffering and pain. Immediately he set to work on a private, secret stone carving, toiling long into the night. Visitors to the shop over the next few days were astounded to see a remarkable likeness of little Caddy taking shape in stone under the hammer and chisel of the wandering carver.

Tombstone of
Caddy Nagle

To this day no one is quite sure how the stranger was able to make such a remarkable likeness of Caddy. Perhaps he had found a photograph of the dear little girl. Or maybe he spoke to the family's friends and neighbors, gathering as much information as possible on John's pride and joy. But at any rate, soon the carving was completed. It showed Caddy standing by the gate, waiting for her father just as she had done so many times in life. The carver then gave his creation to the Naugles, who gratefully placed it on Caddy's grave.

Then, as though his mission here was completed, the itinerant mason left Salem as mysteriously as he had arrived. He was never seen again. No one has ever, after all these years, been able to provide the name of the man who carved the statue of the little girl at the gate.

I arrived at Crown Hill late in the afternoon, just as a storm threatened to break loose. It is a well-tended cemetery, with a mixture of new markers and old headstones. A fresh wind was blowing across the mown grass, and the flowers rustled in the rising breeze.

I wasn't quite sure where Caddy's marker was, and as there was no one available to ask, I set to exploring. Crown Hill is a fairly large place, and it is easy to miss one marker among all the stonework. But just as I was about to head for home, I noticed the small stone figure of a little girl beckoning to me, waiting by a gate as if watching a summer sunset.

Caddy looks just, I'm sure, as she did in real life. Her gentle face peeps over the swinging gate, her little dress draping about her as she waits for her father's return. I felt a deep sense of beauty, of sadness at youth gone so soon, and of serenity. That small face of stone held more answers than any four-year-old's face I had ever seen before.

Tucked in her hands, and in the crook of her arm, was an array of flowers, bright and vibrant against the flat grey statue. With a word of respect and a silent request for forgiveness, I gently moved them to one side so as to better photograph the little girl. And when all was finished, the flowers were placed lovingly back into just the position where I found them. It took me by surprise to find such tender care reserved for so old a marker, neglected as they usually become with the passage of a hundred years.

Caddy does not haunt the cemetery. She is no doubt at peace, playing in endless fields of sunlight and grass, reunited with the father for whom she so devoutly waited at the gate. But the carver remains a mystery. Who was he? Where did he vanish to? And where did he perfect the exacting talent which was demonstrated in the eternal beauty of Caddy's marker. Was he a journeyman stonecutter, perfecting his talent and trade? Or did he come from someplace altogether different, the devoted foster father and craftsman from so many centuries ago, giving back love to a family that had so freely given it to their precious and so deeply missed little girl.[10]

The Weeping Tombstone

Irwin Yoder was not quite 24 years of age when he was laid to rest in Elkhart County's Union Center Cemetery near what is now the intersection of County Road 11 and County Road 50 in November, 1903. His epitaph was a fond farewell to those who knew and loved him:

> "Farewell, Dear Friends,
> From Thee I Am Gone.
> My Sufferings Now Are O'er.
> My Friends Who Knew and Loved Me,
> Will Know Me Here No More."

One would hope that once laid to rest, crime ceases to be a concern to the departed. After all, with neither possessions nor body left to harm, why worry? Yet unfortunately, crime can come even to a cemetery. For Irwin Yoder's rest was disturbed after he was retired to eternal slumber.

For some unknown reason, midnight hooligans with mischief and vandalism on their minds took a hammer to the tombstone, striking the image of Irwin repeatedly. No one knows why, and no one was ever apprehended for the damage. If you look closely at the marker, you can see the darkening under Irwin Yoder's eyes, dark smudges from the grave itself. Mysteriously, the darkening appears just where tears would have fallen from his eyes. Most folks would say it's just moisture, a bit of discoloration down deep in the cracks left by the vandals' hammer. But others know better. Irwin Yoder wept from beyond the grave the night his tombstone was desecrated, his tears leaving bitter marks on the stone surface for all to see.[11]

The Tombstone Lights

One mysterious graveyard, the Pleasant View Cemetery in Prairie Township in Kosciusko County, continues to mystify local residents. On dark, lonely nights, looking from a knoll just south and east of the graveyard, many people have spotted a mysterious luminous light, dancing just above the ground, apparently emanating from a simple dark headstone set by itself in the graveyard. It must be a shy apparition, for the glow always seems to fade into nothingness just as curious investigators approach. The eerie glow has only been glimpsed at a distance, as if whatever kicks up its heels there in the night wishes to be left alone.

At first, it would be easy to write off the occurrence as the reflection of passing automobile headlights bouncing off the smooth, worn stone. Or better yet, the full moon on a cloudless night could reflect its luminous light off the reflective marble surface of some marker. But the Pleasant View lights have been seen on cloudy, overcast nights just as readily as clear ones, and after cars pass by on nearby roads, the glow remains, unaffected by the vehicles passing.

Some researchers wonder if the lights could be caused by some type of magnetic disturbance. Could these tombstone lights be similar to the baffling Marfa lights from the south-

The home of the dancing lights in Kosciusko County

west, another set of mysterious glowing orbs seen only from a distance and only at night?

Other local residents have suggested the lights may be a rare occurrence of 'swamp gas,' sort of like an Indiana will-o-the-wisp. And although cases of luminous gas have been documented in other parts of Kosciusko County, Prairie Township does not have one case of the bizarre natural phenomena on its books, so the mystery remains.

In mid-afternoon my photographer and I arrived at the cemetery. It is a small affair, neatly trimmed and steeped in history. Many of the markers go back well into the 1850s, and a good number of graves were for young men who died in the 1860s. We wondered if these could be Civil War graves, young men plucked in their prime from the heart of a country deep in civil strife. Heaven knows there are enough haunted Civil War sites to fill volumes. Could this be another such place?

There was an air of sadness there, a lonely watchfulness on that small crest of a hill. We paused here and there, taking pictures and remarking about this marker or that wording, when suddenly we were both brought up short by a small, sharp click emanating from behind us, the sound of a stick striking polished marble, or the sound of a hammer being cocked on a Springfield rifle. We both spun around quickly, but could find no cause of the strange sound. Maybe nothing more than the wind disturbing a loose headstone. Maybe not. But we both grew uneasy after that, and wrapped up our work rather quickly, both anxious to be off and away.

Perhaps there is nothing more to the ghostly lights than the by-product of biodegrading indigestion, luminous traces of methane wafting upwards in the night air. Sure, maybe the headlights could reflect just a certain way, depending on the make and model of the vehicle. But none of that could explain that sound we heard, the smallest of sounds, or the uneasiness that settled over us from that point on. I certainly can't explain it. But maybe, if you sit out late one night on North 200 West Road, you might catch a glimpse of the lights rising and flitting about, the dead rising to dance again in the dark beneath a moonless sky in Kosciusko County.[12]

McHarry's Unrest

This story begins in Louisville, Kentucky, in the early 1800s when a young riverman decided to invest in river commerce. He wanted to amass a fortune, marry well, and make a name for himself along the length of the Ohio River. He was Captain Francis T. McHarry, and he was destined to become a legend in his own time.

Captain McHarry, an Irish immigrant, saw the wisdom of investing in growing businesses on the river. He found ways of putting his money in young concerns, like the Portland Canal for example, which was at that time privately owned. Yet he also started many new business ventures on his own. He was the owner of a grain mill in the Portland area of Louisville. He ran a ferry service between Louisville and New Albany. He was awarded the first contract for canals around the falls, and his activities included ownership of the steamer *Music*, a fine riverboat built at the Howard Shipyards in Jeffersonville. She was launched in 1843 and plied the waters of the Ohio River for many years.

The generally accepted story of his demise in historical circles is that he was stabbed while breaking up a violent fight aboard the *Music*. The wounds caused him great suffering and his eventual death. But prior to his passing, he demanded he be buried upright with his eyes open, in a hilltop tomb from where he might witness the river commerce, and vent his bitterness over his demise on the passing boats below. It was even rumored that McHarry had also wanted to be placed in a barrel of whiskey, so to better pass eternity, but that much, at least, never transpired.

When Captain McHarry died on February 15, 1857, his last wishes, minus the whiskey barrel, were fulfilled by his family and friends. They built a huge limestone mausoleum atop Beeler Hill about ten miles below New Albany overlooking the Ohio River. It was built into a limestone outcropping four hundred feet about river level, with the work done in part by slaves. The mausoleum facade itself is an awesome pile of rock. There are several hundred blocks of probably five hundred pounds each, perfectly shaped and fitted into their spots with precision and care. The front wall is over forty feet wide and twenty feet high. The words from McHarry's headstone read,

"When You Are Called,
To Meet Your Friend,
Love Endure, and Sabbath Never End."

The mausoleum still stands today, abandoned and decaying, perched high on the Indiana hillside like some carrion bird watching over the river below, waiting for the next death to feed upon.

But despite the wonderful workmanship and McHarry's precise instructions, his remains were removed from the tomb in 1888 upon the death of his wife, and placed next to hers in the Irwin Mausoleum in Cave Hill Cemetery in Louisville. Yet something of the old captain remains, for despite the absence of his body, many a riverboat captain for years has swore to the existence of balls of light and swirls of white mist emanating from the open doorway to McHarry's tomb. To this day, passersby and townsfolk all know as truth that Captain McHarry is still there, watching over the river that brought about both his fortune and demise, hurling his curses down at the boats that still ply the waters in trade.[13]

The Witch's Throne

Perhaps one of the elements that makes graveyards so decidedly spooky is the neglect that many of the earlier country plots have fallen into. Often one may take a leisurely stroll through a new piece of woods and stumble, literally, onto the remains of one such site. Yet this neglect is not always the case. A remarkably well-preserved graveyard is Stepp Cemetery, situated deep in Morgan-Monroe State Forest. Three miles east of the forest entrance, on Old State Highway 37, Stepp Cemetery stands on a slight rise about a hundred yards north of the main park road. The picturesque nature of the cemetery has been commented on over the years by many locals. And apparently, the dead find it just as attractive.

The history of Stepp Cemetery is clouded in some mystery. Park personnel hold that the cemetery served families who farmed the area before the government's acquisition of their land. A more intriguing account of the cemetery's past goes like this . . .

Stepp Cemetery was connected with the Crabbite religious sect, a fundamentalist group given to such practices as snake handling. The services of the Crabbites were marked by enthusiastic lowering of inhibitions, including but not limited to ritual sexual practices as part of their worship services. The area around Stepp Cemetery, sometimes called the "Precinct," enjoyed an unsavory reputation during the early years of the twentieth century.

Supposedly, once many years ago, a woman in the area of the Morgan-Monroe State Forest had a child which was hit by a car and killed. She buried her child in Stepp Cemetery and had the tree next to the grave cut down and paid for the stump to be carved into a chair so that she might sit in it and guard her child against any strangers that might enter the cemetery. She would sit in her hand-hewn throne, dressed all in black, her long stringy white hair trailing down from her head, rocking the spirit of her little girl.

As a protection for the final resting place of her beloved little girl, the woman placed a curse on her hand-carved throne. If anyone other than the mother were to sit on the hewn stump, the violator would die one year to the day from when they first touched the chair.[14]

Another variant of the Stepp Cemetery haunting dates back to 1957, when a distraught young mother lost her only infant, and shortly thereafter, began the slide towards insanity. Every night she would come dressed all in black to the cemetery and dig up the child, cradling it in her arms in the darkness, as if easing its sleep. Come daybreak, she would place the body back in the coffin and rebury it.

To add to the believability, the baby's grave never settled and grass would not grow there for as long as ten years after the child's death. To further add spice to the tale, lightning struck a large tree next to the grave and left a stump that formed a natural chair. Many people claim to have seen the lady in black rocking her infant while seated in the natural chair.

Stepp Cemetery is indeed a pretty, quiet, out-of-the-way place. Towering pines and stately walnuts overlook the grassy glade, planted here and there with lilies, roses, yucca and other decorative shrubs. There can't be more than six or seven different family names represented there, but there certainly are some interesting markers. I couldn't find a stump carved into the shape of a chair, or a child's grave that would correspond to the sightings there. But there is a low, large, blackened stump, heavily weathered and charred as if hit by lightning, that protrudes from the ground just to the right of the first set of markers. I couldn't be certain that this stump was one and the same as the witch's throne, but nevertheless I took no chances. I did *not* sit on it.[15]

A Ghost's Best Friend

Anyone who has had a devoted pet in their lives knows how deep the affection can run between master and furry friend. There is a story told of the rainbow bridge, a bridge that all pets cross after they die. There they find sunlit fields, plenty of space to run and play, and food and cool water to their hearts content. And they remain there, playing in comfort and warmth, until their own beloved owner crosses to the other side, where they are joined once again in eternal bliss. But what happens when it is the beloved master that passes away first?

In Terra Haute, at the Highland Lawn cemetery, is the Heinl Mausoleum. And just past the stained glass panels of its door, one can glimpse more than the stone bier of death. Rather, you come face-to-face with a pair of bright green eyes, resolutely guarding the rest of John G. Heinl.

John Heinl and his beloved little bulldog, Stiffy Green, were a common sight about the streets of Terra Haute. The two were inseparable and shared a unique bond. John lavished attention on Stiffy, and Stiffy never let John out of his sight, always ready to jump to his master's aid and protection. But unfortunately, all good things come to an end.

John died in 1920, and was laid to rest in his mausoleum. Stiffy was inconsolable. He refused to leave the doors of the mausoleum, and when anyone attempted to take him back to his home, he would snarl and snap, resolutely defending his master's final resting place. He would neither eat nor drink, and finally one morning he was found laying up against the doors, never to move again.

The Heinl family, so moved by Stiffy's undying loyalty, had his body taken to a taxidermist, where he was preserved and mounted so that he could be interred with the master he

The Heinl Mausoleum

loved so much. Now one might shed a sentimental tear and think that would be the end of it. Oh no. Far from it.

After Stiffy's death, strange things began to be noticed about Highland Lawn. Off in the distance, though never from any particular direction, just somewhere distant, many visitors have head the particular bark of a bulldog. Not an angry bark, but one of joy, full of play. And shortly after the barking, people have often heard the voice of a man quietly hushing his four-footed companion.

At other times since 1920, many a person has glimpsed a faint figure of a man strolling about the cemetery, a small dog in tow. From all accounts, the two never pay any attention to anyone about them. They just seem to be enjoying the exercise. And often when the figure is spotted, cemetery workers had seen the doors to the Heinl Mausoleum standing wide open, ready to receive the pair when they are done with their afternoon romp.

Many people over the years have stolen a peek through the door and seen the little bulldog standing still next to his master's resting place. He stares back at them, his bright green eyes glinting in the darkness of the grave, daring them to make a move against his beloved one. As the outsiders move on, so do Stiffy's eyes, following them back and forth, until they think better of disturbing his master's rest and leave.

There are many who say Stiffy is only a statue, nothing more than a loving gesture from a bereft family touched by the little dog's loyalty. But if you have ever heard the legends of the golems of Germany, or the gargoyles in France, you know that statues can, in fact, have lives of their own. And any interference on our parts may have everlasting consequences. I think next time I visit Highland Lawn, I might take a stick along, just in case it's needed for a rousing game of fetch.[16]

Reach Out and Touch Someone

Another story from Highland Lawn Cemetery in Vigo County involves a very frightened man. Death and sleep give similar appearances to the outside world. How many times have you been so exhausted that you used the expression, "I'm just dead"? For Martin Sheets, death was an obsession.

He could see himself, lying on his bed, asleep, while the doctor pulled the covers over his head saying, "I'm sorry, we did all we could." Martin must have had quite an active imagination because that fear went even further. Martin Sheets could hear the church service, he could feel the darkness as the casket lid closed for the last time. He could feel the reverberations as shovelfuls of dirt struck the casket. In his mind he would gasp for breath as the last air in his coffin was used up and he would then slowly die from suffocation.

Now to us, in the safe and comfortable 1990s, we can hardly imagine the chance of being buried alive. But consider the past.

It was not unheard of for a misdiagnosed deceased fellow to sit bolt upright in his coffin during his own wake. Rather than being dead, he had suffered a stroke, or been in a deep coma, his pulse so faint that it seemed nonexistent. It is easy today to check for just such things, but back then, it was not such an unreasonable fear.

So real were these fears for poor Martin, he made sure he had an escape route should he awaken after others thought him dead and gone forever. He had a custom-designed coffin built that could be unlocked easily from the inside, and he had a mausoleum constructed so that he would not have six feet of impenetrable earth above his head if he did awaken from his slumber. The mausoleum would protect him, he thought, but it would also imprison him should he be too weak to attract the attention of the few visitors who graced the cemetery's grounds.

The Sheets Mausoleum

But Martin Sheets was a resourceful man. He had a solution for that problem as well. He installed a telephone with a direct line to the main office of the cemetery, so help could be summoned by lifting the receiver. The line was tied into an automatic indicator light, so that no words had to be spoken. When the Sheets' light came on, help would be on the way.

Death finally came to Martin Sheets, as it does to all men. And for several years operators at the Telephone Central went about their business, although they couldn't help but glance at the Sheets' light from time to time, wondering what they should do if the light ever sprang into life. Times changed and so did the phone system. The direct line was removed, but due to very specific instructions in Martin Sheets' will, the telephone in the mausoleum remained connected and active.

One day many years later, Martin's widow was found lying on her bed, dead. In her hand she clutched a phone so tightly that it had to be pried from her fingers to be placed back on the handset. Her family wondered who she had been trying to call. They imagined her realizing that a stroke perhaps was disabling her, and trying at the last second to call for help. Preparations were made for a quiet service for the woman. When workers went to prepare her place in the mausoleum, everything was normal. Nothing was disturbed, except for one important item. The phone, locked inside, away from the living, was off the hook.[17]

Sister Sarah

One need only mention the name 'Sister Sarah' in Fulton County to any of the longtime residents to get an immediate reaction. There are many varied tales about who Sister Sarah was, or might still be. Some claim she was a nun who killed orphans, and others claim she was a witch. A variety of tales tell of an unwed pregnant woman who threw herself out of a bedroom window, either in desperation, or to escape the fires set by her fiancé to destroy her and the unborn child that was not his.

Sarah's spirit is said to haunt her grave, and every year, many a teen tries to summon forth the restless woman. The list of summoning tricks is long. If you call her name over her grave, located in the Daniel M. McIntire Cemetery, she appears in a puff of smoke. If a glass of water is poured over her grave, and the empty glass is left, it will be found filled with blood half an hour later. She roams the cemetery with a lit candle, woeful and full of remorse for her lost life. Yet perhaps there is even more compelling evidence on Sister Sarah.

Robert Bradway, who lived with his family in the old McIntire home, knows definitively that something unseen—well, usually unseen—walks the halls of the old home. He is not sure that the ghost is Sarah, but he knows for sure that someone is there. He and his wife named their apparition 'Sarah' after seeing the name on the gravestone in the family plot. He knows what he heard on a nightly basis, and what he twice saw.

One evening, he and his wife were asleep in bed, when they both became restless and awoke, sensing immediately that someone, or something, was in their bedroom watching them. There, staring at both of them, was an apparition with long hair and a light-colored robe. Robert couldn't see the face, and actually could only tell the figure was female from the long flowing hair.

"She didn't really glow," he said. "She was an image, a shadow, and yet she wasn't. Within an instant she was gone. We never moved, just looked at her as she floated out the door."

The second time Robert saw Sarah was immediately after he had heard noises upstairs late at night. Thinking that one of his five daughters might be up when she should have been asleep, he determined to sneak upstairs and catch her in the act. Instead, he caught Sarah. She was standing in the hallway, again with the long hair and light-colored robe. And just as quickly, she was gone, fading from view.

"None of us were ever alarmed or afraid," Robert said. "We never had any real problems with her and we never left lights on because we were afraid."

In fact, the only times Sarah has made a nuisance of herself was when she overturned a Christmas tree one night because it was in her 'territory.' Thinking that the family dog might have been responsible, Robert checked on his whereabouts, and found he had been chained outside all night, with no access to the house. Sometimes she would hang pictures face down on a shelf, for no apparent reason.

Family records are inconclusive as to who the specter might be. There were no less than three Sarah McIntires, so identification is difficult. Legend has it that it was Sarah Hoover, married to Richard McIntire, who jumped to her death on November 4, 1873, at the age of thirty-eight.

More than likely, we will never know if 'Sister Sarah' who haunts the house on Fort Wayne Road, and the McIntire cemetery, is Sarah Hoover, one of the other Sarahs, or someone altogether different. Let's just say that I, for one, will not be pouring water over Sarah's grave.[18]

> *As a note, I would ask you to please not visit the McIntire Cemetery to view for yourself the grave of 'Sister Sarah.' The family has for some time had problems with teens visiting in the wee hours of the night, and inadvertently causing damage. This is one specter we all should leave in peace.*

Breaking the Chain of Life

One tale of the unexplainable actually resulted in a government investigation, long before the Fox network and Chris Carter dreamed up the *X-Files*. The story centers around the grave of a man named Pruett, who lies buried in the Orangeville Cemetery. Pruett, a rather hotheaded man, came home early one night from a hard day of work and an even harder night of drinking. He quietly undressed, so as not to wake his wife and risk her ire about his condition. He crept to the bedroom and indeed found her in bed, but not by herself. Enraged, he grabbed a length of chain from somewhere in the house, and after chasing the other man out the door, Pruett strangled his wife to death with the metal links.

Granted, crimes of passion are not that uncommon. But signs from beyond the grave are. Shortly after his burial, a pattern began to appear on Pruett's headstone. A discoloration rather than an etching or a growth, a light yet discernible chain began to form across the surface of the marble, first across the width, then down the length, until an entire cross of chain was forged in the shadows. Locals swore that each full moon added another link to the cross.

Local residents were so convinced of the validity of the tale that it sparked curiosity in some far away Washington D.C. office and two field investigators were dispatched to determine the facts of the strange occurrence. When the agents arrived at the cemetery, one was immediately sarcastic and made fun of the whole notion of "ghosts" while the other man remained quiet as they began their investigation.

After the agents had made their tests and taken photographs, they loaded up their gear and got in their car. The sarcastic agent, now behind the driver's wheel, noticed in his rearview mirror a strange light coming from the tombstone they had just tested.

Driving away, he watched behind him as the lights followed the car. He laughed at the idea, knowing that the image had to be the reflection of his own car lights off a reflective surface. Yet something was gnawing at his brain, and he began to feel that the lights were gaining on him. As he stomped down hard on the accelerator, his partner pleaded with him to slow down, but to no avail; he was running for his very life.

The supernatural chase ended when the car crashed between two roadside posts and rolled over several times. The agent who had been the passenger was thrown clear of the wreck and only slightly injured. But when he went to his partner's aid, who remained trapped within the vehicle, he found him dead—not of his injuries, but from being strangled by a chain that had been strung between the two posts and which had snapped through the windshield and wound itself tightly around the poor man's neck, twisting from him his last breath.

Residents claim that the chain reappears from time to time, and that the federal agent, the second victim of the Pruett's chain, wanders the lonely stretch of highway, desperately looking for a ride to speed him on his way back to his Washington D.C. office, there to file his final report.[19]

Leonora

In the early settlement days of South Bend, a strange shadow fell over what should have been a great occasion for a particular pioneer family. It seems the family had fallen into some good fortune, and had managed to purchase a piece of land in what is now Chapin Park on which to build their new home. Work was begun in earnest, starting with the digging of a root cellar. But as the dirt was removed from the growing excavation, an unnerving discovery was made. The family discovered that the piece of land they had purchased for their home had once been an Indian cemetery. Amongst the dirt lay the remains of several markers of stone, which would indicate there had been European influence at some time, possibly during the French and Indian War.

One marker in particular was in remarkable shape, having been cut from a section of thick hard stone. It had the name "Leonora" etched deeply into its surface. Well, times being what they were, and the family being of a rather pragmatic nature, why waste such a good piece of stone, they figured. After all, it was in such nice shape, cut in such nice rectangular lines and all. Rather than break it up, the family decided to use the old marker as the landing slab for the back doorstep into their new home.

When the family finally moved into the house, they quickly realized that someone, or something, else had moved in with them. A filmy, misty figure was often seen moving quickly down the hall or darting around the corner. Whoever their uninvited guest was, and despite her many sightings, she seemed determined to not let the family ever get a good look at her. She was not a bad ghost. She never upset objects, rattled doors in the night or made a nuisance of herself. In fact, she never seemed to want to frighten anyone. She would scurry out of sight as soon as someone caught a glimpse of her. And except for her extreme shyness, she simply acted as if she were a part of the family and belonged there.

Slowly the family gleaned bits and pieces of information on who their ghostly tenant might be. Old timers said that years ago, Leonora had been an Indian princess who had deeply loved a particular Indian brave (I suppose the princess took a European name at some point, hence Leonora). Unfortunately, the object of her affections did not return her feelings. Leonora was heartbroken, and lived out her life unhappy and alone. Perhaps, the family wondered, Leonora was now seeking with them in their new home the happiness she had so desperately wanted in life.

Well, as all things must, the back door landing began to show signs of wear and use. And when it became apparent that the stone would not survive another harsh winter, the family removed it and replaced it with a new slab of the non-cemetery variety. And it seemed that it was more than the house Leonora was tied to. For once her marker was removed and discarded, her ghost vanished and was never seen by another living soul ever again.[20]

CHAPTER FOUR

DEATH PAYS A VISIT
Figures of Death, Harbingers of Doom

The ancient Greeks, as well as many other cultures, believe that death is more than a cessation of life. The figure of an underworld ruler, or a "grim reaper" figures heavily in many folk tales. Even Charles Dickens was so moved by the image of death that his 'Ghost of Christmas Yet to Come' was seen as skeletal, black-robed figure much like that of Charon, the ferryman on the mystical river Styx. Perhaps the ancients knew more than we give them credit for today . . .

The Fires of Death

Steve Olsen, from northwest Indiana, has grown up in a household where many tales of the unexplained have been handed down by his grandfather, Isaac. Isaac has experienced many bizarre events in his long life, and is reluctant to talk much these days about them. But there was one event that left such an impression on him that to this day he remembers it with vivid clarity.

Isaac and his wife had a large, loving family. And like any parents, they were always concerned if one of their children could not sleep well. So it was not uncommon for one of the little ones to crawl in bed with mother and father, seeking comfort in the dark hours of the night. This was an event well-known and fondly remembered by Isaac. Except one night, something other than one of his children crawled into bed.

One dark evening, after Isaac and his wife and laid down for the night, he felt the end of the bed sag beneath the weight of someone climbing into bed with them. Not thinking much of it, he wondered to himself which child it might be, and what kind of bad dream they might have had. He waited for the

child to say something as it moved up the bed, disturbing mattress and covers, but after a brief silence, Isaac felt an adult hand come to rest on his shoulder. The figure stopped and reclined full length in the middle of the bed, between himself and his wife, who was sound asleep.

Isaac still did not believe anything was truly amiss. Surely it must be one of the uncles or aunts who shared the house with them. Perhaps the radiator in their bedroom had gone bad, and they were seeking warmth. For the hand was large, and ice cold, with a grip as tight as anything he had ever felt. So great was the weight in bed that Isaac could not turn around to see what had hold of his shoulder. He soon learned the frightening reality, however, when a deep, slow voice, with just a slight crack, as if from years of disuse, slowly said, "I am Death."

Isaac froze in terror. He could not move, roll out of bed. He tried desperately to yell to his wife, but no sound came from his throat. He lay there, helpless, in the grip of Death, until the unseen weight moved back to the foot of the bed and vanished.

Isaac did not sleep well the rest of the night, and he prayed to God that the incident was isolated and over. But there was one final page to be played in the drama. At breakfast the next morning, still shaken from what had happened that night, he glanced through the local paper, his eyes coming to rest on the headlines. Apparently in the middle of the night, there was a terrible fire a block away at an orphanage. Most of the children were tragically killed by the inferno. Isaac knew at once that the figure in bed with him had been Death Incarnate, on its way to the orphanage, to collect the lost souls of the little children and ferry them to the other side of the veil.[21]

A Bad Habit

Men in black have become a popular figure of speculation lately. Reported all across the country, these figures, dressed all in black and looking all too much like a living shadows, roam and prowl our streets and byways. Many a motorist have spotted one along a roadside in the rearview mirror, only to take a second look and find the figure gone. Some people have even postulated that these figures are somehow linked to UFOs and alien abduction. But there are more dark figures roaming Indiana than the standard man-in-black. This particular twist on a darkly-dressed apparition has hopefully been sent on into the light, but only time will tell.

There are many who claim that a portrait can capture the soul of a person. Some aboriginal tribes have taboos against photographs, convinced that the device will suck away the living essence of the subject. How many paintings, as you pass by them in some gallery, seem to follow and watch with roving eyes? In the "Portrait of Dorian Grey," a painting reflected the moral deterioration of a man who, to all outward appearances, remained unchanged over the years. And some paintings are full of such life and vibrance that many a critic has made the claim, "the artist put a part of his soul in that work!" At St. Mary's of the Woods, there is a similar story which involves a Sister of Providence who was trapped by her own skills.

This particular nun was a first-rate artist who made portraits her specialty. Her subjects would always look at the final product and say, "That's the real me!" Her secret was to paint the face last, because she felt the face was the true reflection of the person. Hair could change shape and color, but the look of the eyes, the cock of the head would always show their true selves through the hours it took to complete one work of art.

One day the nun decided to do a self-portrait, a decision she would come to regret for all eternity. Everything went well at the start. Her habit was in place, the background filled in nicely. The only part remaining was the face.

That's when fate stepped into the picture. The sister started feeling ill. It became an impossible task to even pick up a brush, let alone use it with the same skill she had wielded in the past. She was taken to the infirmary where, despite the best care from doctors and nurses, she passed away.

That should have been the end of the story, but it wasn't. The incomplete portrait would keep her in this world longer than she would have wished. Not long after her death another sister was praying in the chapel when she heard sobbing. She looked around. There was only one other person in the chapel, another nun. Wanting to help, she approached to ask what was wrong. The figure had its head in its hands, but when it looked up, there was what appeared to be a nun in full habit— minus a face. Just blank nothing.

The other nun went running for help, calling for assistance. But by the time help arrived, the faceless nun was gone. That was not the only time the faceless nun was seen. From time to time she appeared to other sisters and students at the college. Sometimes, in the quiet hours of the morning and evening, she would only be heard, sobbing in the depths of the buildings at the college, her cries echoing down the long corridors. It took an exorcism to free her from her ties to St. Mary's of the Woods. Everyone hopes that she has moved on into the next existence. After all, if she had spent her earthly life worshiping God, then it would be only fitting that her eternal reward be just as sweet. Yet every now and then, if you are alert, you might just catch an echo from her agony over a portrait left unfinished. Perhaps, though moved on, you might one evening catch her visiting her old haunts.[22]

The Demon of Devil's Backbone

Devil's Backbone, a twisting, sharp, and treacherous section of State Road 25 just south of Warsaw, got its name from another undead denizen of Indiana. Back in the 1800s, a farmer was driving his team of horses along a dirt path southwest of Warsaw near Palestine. The farmer came to a winding portion of the road. Along the side was a deep sinkhole that many believed to be bottomless.

It is not known why, but somehow the horses became spooked as they neared the sinkhole area. The farmer was unable to calm them and the horses bolted, stumbling and crashing into the pit, all of them never to be seen alive again.

The sheriff and town's people searched the area for days. Large dragging hooks were used in hopes of catching parts of the wagon, farmer, or horses along the bottom of the neighboring swamp, in case they had plunged in there. But everyone knew what had happened. The hapless farmer had been dragged down into the bottomless pit. No signs were ever found of the poor man, and eventually the residents gave up. Children were warned the area was dangerous and if they slipped and fell in, they would be swallowed up like the farmer and his team of horses.

To this day, the swamp still remains with the road curving and twisting around it. That small portion of the road has been called Devil's Backbone ever since. Many residents have seen over the years a black figure of a man standing near the pit, beckoning them closer. Many have also heard unearthly cries of torment and mournful wails emanating from the depths of the black hole. Some say the cries of anguish come straight up from Hell itself. Others say it's the voice of the farmer, beckoning you to join him in his endless fall, a black figure of doom leading towards damnation.[23]

The Girl in White

I have seen this type of story many times, and usually it is classified as an urban myth. Yet I include one version for your approval. It was heavily documented on the front pages of many newspapers in 1937—more so than the run-of-the-mill myth varieties with which I so often come in contact.

The story began when two WPA officials driving south on U.S. 31 near Franklin saw a young woman dressed in white and wearing white silk slippers walking near the roadway. Naturally the two officials stopped since it was quite uncommon then, as fortunately it still is today, for a young woman to be out in the early morning hours along a deserted roadway alone.

When asked if she was in need of assistance, she explained that she was on her way to Seymour. The men informed the young lady that they were passing right by there, and that they would be happy to give her a ride. Graciously, the young woman accepted their kind offer. As one gentleman helped her into the back seat, he noticed she was quite pale and her hand clammy, but he passed it off to the fact she had after all been running around without a coat or proper dress, and it was a very cold night indeed.

Over the next hour or so, the young woman was quite talkative and chatted about many of the local landmarks with the men who themselves happened to be quite familiar with Seymour. In fact, she described the house where she lived in such detail that the men both recognized it immediately, having passed it many a time.

As the group pulled up in front of the house, the men turned to the girl. She was gone. Puzzled and bewildered, they were only confused rather than frightened, and guessed perhaps she had quickly jumped out of the car and dashed off into the house without them hearing her. To be sure she was all right, they decided to check at the house.

Despite the early hour of the morning, the men knocked and were greeted by an older woman. Telling her of the young lady, she immediately went into hysterics, and her husband came to the door. After calming his wife, he explained to the men that this was not the first time that strangers had knocked on their door at unusual hours with the same tale. In fact, it had been happening on a regular basis since the death of their daughter five years earlier.

The "Girl in White" of U.S. 31 continues to make her appearances, although they have lessened in number in recent years. Many reports have placed her coming out of a Greenwood cemetery and even going up on the porch of her house and knocking before she vanishes. Whether she exists or not can be argued, but she has become quite famous due to the number of official reports and subsequent newspaper coverage.[24]

The Seance

In my research, I use the resources of the Internet and the World Wide Web quite extensively. Through newsgroups and e-mail, I keep in touch with many people from around the world who have kindly volunteered their own run-ins with the supernatural. One such story came from a young woman named Jean*, a recent graduate of Notre Dame. She related a chilling encounter with lingering death she will not quickly forget. Jean wrote,

"This all happened in 1986-87 while I was living in a two-bedroom apartment near Notre Dame with another friend. Our place was a divided-up older home, and we rented both bedrooms on the second floor. Neither I, my roommate nor any of my friends did drugs or anything like that, so what happened definitely wasn't any kind of hallucination.

Ashley*, my roommate, had come in one night and informed me that ever since we had moved into the house, she had had a difficult time going into our bathroom, which had doors leading to it from both bedrooms. She said she felt extremely uncomfortable in there. I had never noticed anything, but then I spent little time in the house since my studies kept me at school so much.

For some reason, Ashley suggested we have a seance to see if anything was in the house. None of us knew what we were doing, but Ashley knew someone who claimed he did, and invited him to come to the house on a Friday night. I was pretty open to it, although extremely skeptical about anything happening. I was sure it was just a case of nerves on Ashley's part.

Anyway, one Friday night, he and two friends of ours showed up with Ashley, and though I don't remember how we got everything ready, I do remember that Aaron*, the lead person, had us make sure all the windows in the house were closed. He also had us put a towel against the base of the bathroom window (to make sure there were no drafts). He then he lit a large candle which he made sure was firmly in the holder we had provided. He stood and watched it for awhile and then set it down in the empty dry bathtub.

We closed both doors and all went out into the now candle-lit living room. He had us all hold hands, and Aaron attempted to speak to whoever or whatever might be in the house. He asked for a confirmation that someone or something was in the bathroom—he wanted the candle, which was brand new, to be extinguished, and he was trying to either get this thing out of the bathroom or at least allow it to leave.

Nothing seemed to happen for awhile, but then this rather creepy (and for lack of better words) low inaudible buzzing, humming noise started. It was more like it was some kind of low electrical current flowing through all of us—as if you could hear and feel it *inside* as well as *outside* your body at the same time. I found it very uncomfortable and wanted to let go of my friends' hands, particularly my roommate's hand who was sitting to my left. I think others were feeling the same sensations because it wasn't long after that I started hearing others in the group whispering. After the group started whispering, the humming stopped.

None of us felt very comfortable and even our conversation seemed forced. We all were feeling like something not quite right was happening. Finally, Ashley said in a whisper "look at Molly*" who was a friend of mine sitting on the other side of me. I was almost afraid to look at her, but as I turned my head I noticed she had this dead, vacant stare on her face and was looking towards my bedroom. By then I had dropped her hand and was calling her name. I started to feel a bit frantic when there was absolutely no response or even slight blinking of her eyes. She didn't acknowledge hearing any of us.

Suddenly, she bolted off the couch. Ashley and I took off right behind her. She reached for the bathroom door, but before she could open it, Aaron stopped her and then proceeded to open it slowly himself. There was this cold air that "wooshed" out of the room and felt as if it went right through our bodies as we clustered around the open door, as if we'd just let something or someone out of the room.

The candle, to our shock, was not only out, but had been knocked over, candle holder and all! Just from how it looked we knew there was no way it could have fallen over on its own. Someone would have had to lift it and lay it on its side.

Then Molly, who hadn't uttered a word until then, said "We finally let him out." None of us had a clue what she was talking about, and when asked who "he" was, she had no idea. She said she just knew she had to get to the door and let "him" out.

I was almost terrified to have Aaron and Molly leave, since they were the ones who had sort of unleashed whatever this was on us. There was no other occurrence after that, and for weeks we had no idea who "he" might be.

But then one afternoon as Ashley and I were sitting out on the steps talking about the seance we saw our paperboy, who was about fifteen years old, coming up the street. We thought that perhaps he might know a bit about the history of the house. When we asked, he told us that no one had lived in the house for very long since a guy had overdosed on heroin in the bathroom about six years prior. We both just knew that we'd let this guy out of the bathroom.

I have no idea why or how he was finally freed, but it wasn't long after this conversation with the

paperboy that we decided to move out of the
house. I never returned to the house after our
move, and I have no idea if any other events have
ever happened at that location. I myself never
want to find out.

CHAPTER FIVE

HUMOROUS HAUNTS
Spirits of Delightful Fright

It seems that some ghosts take pride in the pranks they play on the living. Be it watching over their favorite locale or taunting the nonbeliever, there is a rare variety of spirit that, while never truly harmful, should never be mocked. The following account was sent to me by Fred*. He describes the true accounts of a protective spirit during a five-year span of his teenage life in the 1930s.

The Protective Phantasm of Phoebe

Phoebe, in Greek mythology, was a moon goddess portrayed as a virgin huntress. In my life, Phoebe was a virgin spinster huntress who resided in a very old stone and brick building which had formerly been a family memorial library. This building consisted of fourteen rooms; six on the first floor, six on the second floor and two more recently built rooms on the third floor located to the right of the staircase landing and part of an enormous unfinished garret which was entered from the left side of the landing.

This garret was twenty-feet high, covered the entire expanse of the building and contained a loft similar to a hayloft which had been built over the ceilings of the two more recently-built rooms on the right of the landing; a simple, sturdily-constructed wooden twenty-foot staircase without handrails going to a trapdoor in the roof; and a passageway which circled the back and right sides of the two newer rooms. This passageway was paneled with unfinished wood and had a few supposedly secret sliding panels which covered niches used to hide money, jewelry, and other valuables.

Phoebe was the last in a long line of owners, all direct descendents of one another, and when she died, the memorial library was closed. The building had been part residence, part library and with Phoebe's death, the library contents were stashed in two very large rooms on the first floor and all the furnishings and personal belongings were removed from the premises. While none of Phoebe's remaining relatives wanted to live there, they didn't want the stately old building and its grounds of seven acres to be abandoned and vandalized. This family heard that my grandfather, a well-known medical doctor and archaeologist, had just died and my family was going to move from the residence that was also his office, so Phoebe's relatives offered the memorial library building rent free to our family if we would live there and take good care of it. That is how I became acquainted with Phoebe.

Twice a year, my parents, aunts and uncles, and I would clean the entire house, including the garret and the two empty rooms on the third floor. I remember it was in my fourteenth year and while my Aunt Margaret and I were wiping down the walls in one of the third floor plastered rooms that I made a remark that I'd bet old Phoebe never did as good a job as I (frankly, I didn't believe in Phoebe, who was rumored to haunt the house). Just then a slate shingle from the roof flew from somewhere, missed my head by two feet and landed on the floor about six feet from me. Aunt Margaret was busy wiping a wall about three feet on the other side of me and I could tell she was shaken as she asked me to please keep my thoughts about Phoebe to myself. That was the only time in our living there that we found a slate shingle that had become loose. As other events occurred in later years I became convinced that Phoebe never wanted to seriously hurt me, but only wanted a spirited laugh at my expense. That night I heard a low mirthful sound from somewhere on the upper floors and it didn't sound like the wind!

The house had long halls on the first floor and second floors which ran the length of the building. It had no electricity. It had eight fireplaces and four chimneys—two fireplaces to a chimney. About a year after the slate slinging, my Aunt Clara and I were alone in the house. Sometime, after dark, while my aunt and I were reading in the dining room, we heard a noise in the main hall just off the dining room. We were terrified—a burglar? An intruder? An animal? God knows what! We picked up a coal oil lamp and clinging together like two pieces of velcro we tiptoed into the hall. It was empty! The lamp cast huge monstrous shadows of us on the walls, shadows increased in size by our hair standing on end. Suddenly, the noise was behind us. We peeked over our shoulders, bug-eyed, and then saw it, the wing of a chimney swift was protruding from the back of the picture of good old Phoebe! I'd swear the picture had a faint smile. Later that night I heard the amused chuckle again somewhere upstairs. Since all the fireplaces were sealed off, did Phoebe get that chimney swift from the same place she got that roof slate?

Another feature of the house was a covered stone front porch which had twelve stone steps leading up to the main entrance as the residence-library stood on a ridge which gradually slanted down to the road. Under the porch was a wine cellar. And a flock of about thirty or forty pigeons used to roost on the porch roof at night.

One night, we were having a birthday party for my grandmother. My Uncle George was there. He found a couple of feathers lying under Phoebe's picture on the hall floor. Grandma identified the feathers as those of pigeons and told George that she couldn't imagine how they got into the house but informed him of the pigeons on the front porch roof. Upon hearing of the pigeons, George declared that he loved pigeon pie and that he was going right up the front stairs to the windows that opened above the porch roof to see if he could capture a couple. To his surprise, as he peered out the window, he saw an apparent burglar on the porch trying to pry open another window about six feet away. Uncle George had no weapon, but he grabbed a bedsheet, threw it over himself, flung open the door of the room where the other window was located, ran in, and waved his arms wildly. Last seen, the would-be intruder was setting the world's record for the mile run through a distant cornfield. Several of us again swore we heard Phoebe quietly laughing in the garret. Had she planted the feathers in the hall to ward off the impending robbery?

My cousin, Johnny, came to board with us as he had just obtained employment in the vicinity of where we lived. Johnny loved the Fourth of July and fireworks of every kind. On his first Fourth with us, in the late 1930s, he brought four huge shopping bags of fireworks from Kentucky to shoot in the relative seclusion of our back yard. During the day he heard us discussing Phoebe. He scoffed long and loud. About one in the afternoon, Johnny produced a package of four so called "busters"—giant ten-inch long, three-quarter-inch wide firecrackers. They turned out to be a bust for sure, two made less noise than most two-inch regular firecrackers and two merely sputtered and went out.

About eleven-thirty in the evening, after Johnny had put on a gorgeous display of skyrockets, roman candles, aerial bombs , pinwheels and every kind of fountain and sparkler, we retired to the dining room for a late snack. My mom asked my dad if he would go out to the cistern as we were out of water. Johnny accompanied him. While Dad was pumping water, Johnny found the remains of one of the fizzed out ten-inch "busters" from earlier and attempted to break it in half. We, in the dining room, saw a flash like a dozen flashbulbs, heard a roar like a cannon and in the door came Dad, leading Johnny by the hand. Johnny's face, neck and arms were pitch black, his eyebrows were completely gone and he couldn't see a thing. We rushed him to the doctor.

To everyone's amazement, including the doctor's, Johnny's head, face, arms and hands when cleaned off, had no cuts, burns, or bruises. His eyesight returned to normal very quickly, only his eyebrows were gone! Without eyebrows he had a comical appearance. I reminded him that Phoebe never harmed scoffers but she knew how to scare them and put them in their places. Johnny joined the believers!

I should point out that none of my family or relations ever visited the third floor after dark. Just a precaution! At his place of employment Johnny acquired five young respectable male friends who asked our permission to spend a night sleeping in the two unfinished rooms on the third floor of our residence; Johnny would join them so they would sleep three to a room. We agreed.

At first, all went well. Then as night progressed, our guests decided it was cowardly to sleep three to a room. Rather, one apiece would sleep in each of the third floor rooms while Johnny and the other three slept on the landing at the bottom of the stairs leading to the third floor. Greg* drew one room, Harry* the other. Both pretended to sleep, but neither did, as they experienced strange sounds in each of the rooms and felt an unseen presence about them. It was totally dark and both decided they had had enough of the strange noises. Each of them vacated their rooms unbeknownst to the other. Greg was barefooted, tiptoeing, carrying his shoes. Harry was crawling on his hands and knees. At the top of the landing, Harry's hand came down on Greg's bare foot. Greg screamed and kicked furiously, Harry yelled and tackled Greg. Each were both fully convinced that he was under spectral attack, and now was the time to fight for his very life. Over and over they went, down the stairs, punching, clawing, biting, letting out the most god-awful yells. The other four young men, including Johnny, not knowing what was descending upon them, tore down the next flight of stairs, out the front door, and into the night. Eventually Greg and Harry got outside, too. Battered, bruised and bleeding, they discovered their error. Just before dawn, we once again heard in the eaves of the garret sounds like gales of laughter. Because they were invading her private nightly domain did Phoebe cause the noises and sensations that led to Greg and Harry abandoning their posts?

One Sunday, about noon, a Mrs. G. telephoned us—yes, no electricity or plumbing, but we did have a telephone! She indicated that she had been a long-time friend of Phoebe's family and would like to see the old house once again, one last time. After checking her out with Phoebe's family, we were told that Mrs. G. was a nosy busybody, but if we didn't strongly object, would we please accommodate her this one time.

All two-hundred-fifty pounds of this dowager who sneezed like a cat came waddling to our door on that Sunday afternoon. She was bedecked with every kind of bauble and peered at everything through a gold-plated lorgnette! She peeked into every corner and informed us that although she liked Phoebe's family, Phoebe herself was a "pain in the butt." After satisfying her curiosity, and just before leaving, she declared she must use the toilet. We told her we had only two stationary commodes with removable chamber pots located on the second floor, or, if inconvenient, there was an outhouse. She opted for the commodes, but just as she started up the stairs something loudly fell on the second floor, and frightened, she refused to continue. So she turned around and headed for the outhouse. I would like to point out that the entire family was on the first floor at the time of the mysterious crash. We never did learn the source of the noise.

As the outhouse was overdue for emptying, the contents were rather high, in more ways than one.

Mrs. G. entered the outhouse, there was a cracking, a scream, we ran to the outhouse. Mrs. G.'s great weight had broken the framework holding the seats and her prodigious posterior was wedged in, touching the preponderance of post-digested matter below her. Needless to say, she appeared to be in shock. We extricated her and took her to the only doctor we knew would be likely to be home on Sunday, a 75-year-old, mostly retired, crusty character who, having been a good friend of my medical doctor grandfather, would surely help us. The doctor cleaned her up with a disinfectant soap, pulled out some splinters, gave her a shot, and except for a tender tail, she appeared to be in good shape. We never heard from her again.

Returning to the house, we related our adventures to Grandma who observed, "She should never have referred to Phoebe as a pain in the butt, now look who's got the pain in the butt. I bet the noise of something falling we all heard when Mrs. G. started up the stairs was Phoebe's way of redirecting her to the outhouse." That night, the laughter was exceptionally loud in the garret. It seemed the entire house was squeaking with titters of delight.

The house was sold a year later and we moved away shortly thereafter.

CHAPTER SIX

LANTERNS FOR THE DEAD
Mysterious Lights and Glowing Orbs

Many researchers in the paranormal field speculate on the relationship between electrical fields and haunted sights. There seems to be a parallel between electricity, or that which conducts it well, such as bodies of water, and paranormal disturbances. Houses near lakes, rivers, or over underground springs might somehow generate a weak electrical field that can attract or, heaven forbid, trap, the resonances of earthbound spirits. These tales makes one think when that dim and misty light is seen just behind that tree, just rounding the bend ahead.

The House of Blue Lights

Skyles E. Test was a rich, brilliant, eccentric gentleman who owned a house surrounded by vast grounds on what was then the northeast edge of Indianapolis. Test, an inventor and one of the forerunners in the use of solar energy, even installed a solar-heated swimming pool, something unheard of during his time. He also had distinct views on city utilities. He refused to partake in them; rather, he dug his own well and built a private generator to supply all of his electrical needs.

Test was something of a character and considered by many to be more than a little strange, but none could deny that he celebrated the holidays with relish. Neighbors would walk or ride past his property in droves to see the hundreds of orange and black lights on Halloween, the red lights for Valentine's Day and the patriotic red, white, and blue bulbs he strung on the Fourth of July. One would assume his celebration of the Christmas season would naturally include the display of the colors red and green, but this was not the case. At Christmas, Test's entire property vibrated with the glow of cold blue lights.

People had been enjoying Test's array of lights for years, but then one and another began remarking that although New Year's Day and old holiday of Twelfth Night (January 6) had come and gone, the blue lights were still burning from dawn till dusk. Oh well, maybe he was just extending the season to the next holiday, they reasoned. But then Valentine's Day came and still the blue lights burned. Finally, someone suggested it might have something to do with the fact that Test's wife had died an untimely death the year before and perhaps the blue lights had been her favorite, and he was leaving them up in her honor.

Although the death of Mrs. Test did influence her husband's decision to keep the blue lights burning, it was not because they were necessarily her favorite. Test, you see, believed that the color blue attracted the spirits of the dead, and the blue lights were lit each night to help guide the apparition of his departed wife back home.

During the years following his wife's death, Test became even more eccentric, some said downright crazy. He began buying items by the barrel—enough to last a lifetime, perhaps two or three lifetimes. He acquired a large number of cats and dogs as well, for reasons unknown. But what was really weird was that when a member of his menagerie died, he purchased a small coffin in which he laid out the deceased and even made pictures of the dead creature to send to his friends. (The Marion County Public Library has many of these photographs in its basement, if any of you readers would like to see the macabre scenes.)

Stories sprang up around Test, his menagerie, and his bizarre behavior. Locals claimed that Test, who missed his wife so greatly that it warped his mind, had her body preserved and placed inside a sealed glass coffin in the living room. Teenagers would dare one another to go up to the house and look inside the living room windows for the woman resting there in the glass coffin. Just as strangely, these same locals swore that the body of Mrs. Test had somehow been reinvested with her departed spirit, due in part to her husband's efforts with his alluring blue lights, and that she, trapped between death and life, would attempt to go about her daily activities, such as answering the door if a brave soul ventured close enough to ring the bell.

Following Test's death, even though the old place was empty and the electricity, including Test's private generator, cut off, people passing late at night still reported seeing an eerie blue glow emanating from the property.

With the passage of the years, the city decided to raze the dilapidated Test dwelling. Although many history buffs rallied to save it, alas, their efforts were in vain for the contents were auctioned off and the house torn down to make way for a park. When the building was torn down, workers found beneath the basement the entrance to a two-mile-long tunnel Test had apparently built out to the Geist Reservoir. Inside that tunnel they discovered all the barrels of provisions Test had been stockpiling, as well as hundreds of military food ration packs and thousands of dollars of survival equipment.

Those city officials who had been in favor of the demolition of the old place assured themselves and each other, that if nothing else, this would get rid of those damned blue lights and the curious throngs who had nothing better to do than go looking for them. The authorities were dead wrong. Not only did the inquisitive continue their pilgrimages to the site, hoping to catch a glimpse of the mysterious blue lights, many of them were not disappointed, for there, in the distance, the eerie lights still glowed. Lack of electricity, death itself, and even total destruction could not extinguish Test's blue lights.[25]

All Aboard . . . Next Stop, Death

Death can take many forms, from lingering illness to sudden and tragic demise. For the soul, a natural death leads to another existence, a higher plane of being. It is the sudden death that can cause problems, bringing about the refusal of the soul to accept what has happened. Thus, the spirit of the deceased lingers on in familiar surroundings.

A rather disturbing incident involving just one such sudden death occurred in Vigo County, on the north-south railroad mainline. A fast freight train was highballing it, careening down the tracks on its way to Evansville when a trestle gave way, sending the train flying to its sudden and fiery demise. The accident killed both the conductor and the engineer.

The conductor's body was found intact, but the engineer's was another matter—his body was found in the wreckage, minus his head. And try as search crews might, the head was never recovered. Locals now joke that the engineer never could accept death with a good head on his shoulders. Ever since the wreck, strange lights have been seen near the scene of the crash, slowly traveling up and down the tracks, a ghostly lantern swaying in the wind, all in the fruitless search by the engineer for his lost head.

Tortured souls can be put to rest, taught to move on into the next existence, reassured that it's all right to leave. The question remains though . . . does the engineer want to, without his missing head?[26]

The Leesburg Lights

On a lonely road between Leesburg and North Webster, travelers have, from time to time, encountered an inexplicable floating orb of light. The sphere is believed to be harmless as no one has ever come to a dire end from an encounter with the strange will-o-the-wisp. It generally just bobs and dances along paying no mind to the observer. But occasionally, the light gets downright frisky, and may follow viewers as they attempt to leave the area, or even, it's said, chase visitors through its domain. Many have wondered if perhaps this tale started by sightings of ball lightning, an extremely rare atmospheric and electrical disturbance that has been known to fly down chimneys and chase people across the open countryside. Whatever the mysterious lights, they remain a complete mystery.

The Light of Love

The woods east and north of Vincennes University used to be the dividing line between the white settlement and the Indians' tribal lands. According to legend, a white girl and an Indian boy fell in love, much to the chagrin of their respective communities. They were each forbidden to see one another, but, of course, youth being what is is, they ventured into the woods despite the warnings not to rendezvous and spent the night together.

When their respective communities found out they were missing, they were furious. Searchers swarmed into the woods and scoured the countryside. Finally finding the couple, the searchers beat the hapless pair to death, terribly mutilating the bodies in the process. They then hung their bodies from the trees as a lesson to other youngsters never to step out of line.

Now it is alleged that if a young couple in love spends the night in those woods, the angry ghosts of the girl and boy will appear out of the darkness, and in vicious spite, will mutilate the transgressors and then hang the fresh bodies from the trees, a hideous reminder of the love they were so cruelly denied.[27]

A Place to Dry Out

A derelict house from the late-nineteenth century was the focus for a gathering of ghostly lights for many years. Located in Indianapolis on West Merrill Street near the White River, the abandoned two-story structure seemed to be a gathering place for ghosts. On cold, wintery nights, strange mists and glowing orbs were often observed rising from the White River, drifting up the bank, and through the dark windows of the abandoned house. Shortly thereafter, loud low laughter and a kind of song-like moaning would float on the air from the dark recesses of the old building, as if the lights that had entered were engaged in spirited conversation. The sounds would go on far into the night as observers listened intently, yet terrified, from outside.

If the police were called to investigate, the sounds would stop the minute the door was opened. And as soon as the investigating troopers would leave, the revelry would commence again in earnest. In fact, the only person the lights ever allowed to witness their escapades was a brave African-American watchman who would sneak into a closet and watch what went on. He reported of a strange nocturnal assemblage of spirits sitting in a circle in an upstairs room, telling stories far into the night and singing. The night watchman had the distinct impression that these souls were drowning victims who had perished in the White River.

After several years of observation, he noticed one night that the circle had grown. He listened attentively to the wailings of the newest spirit, but could only observe that the voice was that of a female, whereas all the others had been male. He left to tell of his latest find to the firemen at the station house on the corner where he often stopped to chat. While telling the tale, a call came in and the firemen raced to a nearby bridge over the White River. Below, floated the body of a woman who had jumped off the bridge two hours earlier and drowned. It had only taken her a few minutes to join the ghostly group in the house of spirited revelry.[28]

Dixon's Lanterns

Residents in Tunnelton say that the spirit of Dixon, the old night watchman for the train tunnel east of town, still roams the railroad passage.

The story goes back a few generations, before the railroad companies lined their tunnels with brick. A watchman was employed to patrol the tunnel after the passing of each locomotive, to make sure the vibrations from the massive engine had not shaken loose any rock that might be blocking the path. The watchman carried two old-style railroad lanterns, not just to light his own way, but to signal to an approaching train not to proceed.

Delbert Brewer, who lives in Salem, tells how his uncle, Dixon was killed back in 1906 in the tunnel. It seems that a work crew was employed to begin the arduous task of lining the tunnel with bricks. A group of local girls decided to use the railroad tunnel as a shortcut to their houses, and were accosted by a few of the workers. Dixon went into the tunnel to protect the girls, and to make sure they were safely on their way. Dixon must have raised a few hackles with the Italian immigrant workers, for poor Dixon was found a few days later in the middle of the tunnel, his head struck from behind with a pick. Dixon was later buried in Procter Cemetery, next to Dixon Chapel, about three miles north of Fort Ritner, just over the Jackson County Line.

Dixon's great niece, Donna Sanders, remembers the tales her grandmother Daisy told about Dixon and how he returned to his wife, Mary Collier Dixon, after his murder. A picture of Dixon, sitting on a shelf in his and Mary's home, fell over face downward at the instant of his murder. And although Mary tried to re-hang the picture several times, she never could get it to stay upright after that night.

Mary always claimed that Dixon was not dead. She claimed the her loving husband would come back from time to time. She would speak to him often, and he told her that it had indeed been the Italian workers who had done him in. Shortly after Dixon's death, Mary returned home to the Collier house, bringing her children with her, as well as the spirit of her departed husband, who continued to look after his wife. Mary never remarried; rather, she remained the bride of the ghost her beloved Dixon had become.

Many people have seen mysterious lights floating in the dark tunnel. Since the tunnel curves slightly, you can not see completely through from end to end. On a dare, many a teen have braved the tunnel, walking to the midpoint where Dixon was slain. Once there, they have heard ghostly footfalls echoing in the tunnel, coming towards them, and the lights from the railroad lanterns swinging gently beneath an unseen watchman's arms.[29]

CHAPTER SEVEN

GHOST IN THE MACHINE
Ghosts In and Around the Workplace

Just as some people are reluctant to leave the office, so too are the workaholic ghosts that continue to slink around their former workplace, never satisfied with the job done by others, convinced that only their spectral hand can add that perfect final touch.

The Star-Crossed Lovers

Employees of a manufacturing firm in Bedford agree that their work force includes someone, or something, not listed on the payroll. Many workers have felt the touch, the presence of the unseen, yet they remain split on the identity of the invisible occupant of their building.

Robert*, the chief executive officer of the firm, has heard footsteps on several occasions, accompanied with the noises of large objects being moved around in upstairs rooms, yet he is nervous and skeptical towards their ethereal employee. Robert has asked that the name of the business and the nature of its industry not be revealed. After all, who would want a potential customer questioning the credibility of a business which claimed to have a ghost on its payroll.

Many of the employees have found the ghost's antics over the years a hindrance, as objects are moved or tools vanish from known locations. Others feel it is a blessing rather than a hindrance—an unseen night watchman—looking over the old place. Stan*, a longtime employee, thinks he has the whole thing figured out.

He insists that two ghosts, male and female victims of a tragedy, roam the halls, stairs, and attic of the office area, hand-in-hand, seeking unattainable love.

People who have been in the office alone at night or on Saturdays report that they have heard footsteps, doors opening and closing, and heavy furniture being moved around, but no one can be seen. "It's kind of hair-raising," Stan said.

One other employee, Joe*, said he would expect to see his boss come walking through the door to the office following the normal sounds of someone entering the building. But no one would be in the building and no car would be in the parking lot.

One of the most difficult ghostly habits to explain is the mystery of the locked doors. Each night, all doors to the building are locked, and security devices activated. The doors will be checked and verified locked after midnight. But sometimes when workers return in the morning, the doors are unlocked with the security measures still in force.

Who unlocks the doors but doesn't disturb the security system? Can anything other then a specter pass through an electronic system without triggering the alarms? Supervisors have no answer.

Perhaps the most annoying habit of the phantom is that of disturbing tools and machines. At the end of the day, workmen will put their tools in one place, then return to work the next morning to find the tools gone. Invariably the tools show up at another machine or work area.

Changing the setup of a machine has caused unwanted hassles for employees. A person will adjust a machine to manufacture a certain item and run test pieces to be certain the setup is correct before closing down for the day. The next morning the machine will not work as prepared the previous night.

Scotty*, one of the employees who insists that the spirits are helpful actually benefited from the ghost's generosity. He was repairing an old faucet in his home and discovered he needed a part that was no longer available for the ancient plumbing. Remembering that a former owner of the office building once did plumbing, the man decided to search upstairs at the office for old plumbing parts. He hunted around in the upper story, and just as he was about to give up, he heard a noise from over in one corner. Going to investigate, Scotty found tucked in the corner a lone basket containing just one plumbing part, exactly the part he was searching for. "You may call it coincidence," Scotty says vehemently, "but I say the ghost was very helpful. He put it there for me to find."

As for the two lovers who roam the halls, perhaps they are the shades of a young man and woman who were gunned down within the building by a jealous ex-husband. Al*, a company supervisor, pointed at a dusty spot on the floor, the scene of the grisly double murder.

"It was right here . . . it happened here," he said cautiously, as if the very act of identifying the murder scene might bring forth their spirits. "This is where I sense a presence, a feeling we are not alone."[30]

Elmer

Another workplace in Bedford seems to have its share of unusual happenings as well. The employees of this office building think the ghost and his antics are amusing. Most of them laugh as they tell the stories. One employee, however, actually quit his job over the haunting. There are sensible explanations for everything that happens—well, almost everything.

The owner of the building said he doesn't believe in ghosts, not even the one said to haunt his building, but he can't explain it all either. "Please don't identify us. If anyone thought I believed this stuff they wouldn't do business with me."

Apparently the ghost has occupied the building for the more than twenty years the current owner has owned it. Most of the hauntings are the usual noises. One of the owners said, "You hear noises all day long, someone at the door, voices, footsteps, but no one is there." She said the first employee to hear the ghost was a man who believed that buildings could absorb sounds over a period of time, and slowly release these recorded sounds years later. He went so far as to name the spirit "Elmer," so Elmer he has been for more than twenty years. Elmer has no regular habits. He doesn't walk at a certain time or in a certain pattern. There's nothing anyone can pinpoint. And no one knows of any tragedy that occurred at the old limestone building to inspire a ghost, but Elmer's mischief continues.

Early one morning an employee was to meet another man at the building and the two were to take a trip together. The first man let himself into the building to wait for the second. He heard footsteps in the room above where he was standing. He was so frightened that he refused to stay in the building, preferring to wait in the dark and cold outside until his friend came.

Ten years ago, another man, in the same room, heard footsteps going up the stairs right above his office at 5:00 a.m. Whatever it was, it never came back down. He searched upstairs, but found no one.

While doors seem to open and close by themselves, this is not too unusual. What is unusual is the following incident that occurred to the owner's son. At quitting time, the son closed the door to the snack room, where a variety of soda and snack machines are kept for the convenience of the employees. The next morning he had great difficultly shoving the door open. Full, heavy Coke cases had been stacked against the inside of the door, an impossible task to accomplish from the outside, as there is no other door to the room and all windows were locked, from the inside. How did the heavy cases get across the room and against the door from the inside? No one can explain it.

Another son, who keeps an old car in the basement of the building, saw what he described as a vapor or swirling cloud at the bottom of the basement stairs. It is the only sighting of the ghost known to the establishment. The same son, one night when no one else was in the building, saw the intercom light on the telephone light up. Wondering who else was in the building, he went from office to office, but they were all empty. Thinking someone in a nearby building was using the line, he went to the other building, but it was all dark, vacant.

Early in Elmer's career, an employee in the front office heard the front door open and close, but when he checked, no one was up front. The employee returned to the back, when suddenly he felt someone breathing down his back. Then he heard footsteps behind him, but there was no one there.

"About everyone who has worked here has a story to tell. Some people won't stay because of the little things that happen," says the owner. But no harm has been done to anyone and most employees enjoy a good laugh from time to time as they relate the latest stories of Elmer and his tricks.[31]

Spirited Dinner Guests

It's not often that one gets the opportunity to dine with high spirits, especially in a state that is as grounded in good old-fashioned common sense as Indiana. But for guests at Porticos Restaurant in Bloomington, that is exactly what they had the chance to experience on a regular basis. Although the restaurant closed in June, 1992 after twelve years of business, it had a reputation of scaring the appetite out of even the staunchest nonbeliever in the unexplained.

The towering 12,000-square-foot limestone structure, majestically capped by slate shingles, was built in 1890 by Philip Kearny Buskirk, president of First National Bank in Bloomington. The supporting walls are of locally-hewn limestone eighteen inches thick. Multiple fireplaces were installed to heat the building despite the superior insulating qualities of the limestone. Eventually the home was sold to William Graham, who built the Graham Plaza Hotel, and later to William Showers of the Showers Furniture Factory.

The Showers family renovated the imposing 1890s interior. German craftsmen, employed by Showers, installed leaded glass, hand-carved doorways and ceilings, hardwood floors, solid cherry paneling and terra cotta relief decorations. In 1915, the local newspaper recognized this home as "the most beautiful in Bloomington."

In the late 1940s, Phi Kappa Tau fraternity purchased the property, and as time passed, the once-elegant building became home to Toad Hall, a furniture store, and The Whimples of Walnut Street restaurant until finally, in 1980, Dr. and Mrs. Steven Lewallen purchased it as home for the Porticos.

Some novelties of Porticos included a prohibition-era liquor cabinet concealed behind a false wall, a wall safe hidden behind a mirror in the banquet room, and more than its share of unexplained happenings.

The most puzzling, and perhaps the most disturbing, manifestation might be best described as the "disappearing children." The first recorded incident occurred in the mid 1980s when at three in the morning the police called the owners of the restaurant, Steven and Anita Lewallen, with the unsettling news that the alarm company had heard noises in the restaurant through audio monitors connected to the burglar alarm system. According to the alarm company, the system was registering the noises of children bouncing a ball in the second floor hallway and yelling, "Mommy, Daddy, come play with us."

Quickly responding to the alarm, in the event that some unwitting patron's children had inadvertently been locked inside the structure, the police walked inside and flicked on the lights. After an exhaustive search throughout the building, they found that the restaurant was empty.

Another occurrence of the mysterious children centered around a guest at Porticos who started to walk upstairs to use the women's facilities. Shortly after leaving the table, she returned, exclaiming, "I can't get up the stairway. There are some children sitting on the steps with their arms locked and won't let me pass by." Mrs. Lewallen hurried over to the stairway. But not only were there no children blocking the stairs, there were no children in the entire building.

On more than one occasion, dinner guests would come down from the upstairs bathroom and ask, "Are those your kids playing upstairs?" The owners themselves actually got a glimpse of the children one night as the young twosome bounced a ball back and forth to each other. But phantom children are not the only unsolved mystery about Porticos.

Late one evening, after all the guests had left and the restaurant had been locked, the manager, Jim*, and three waiters descended to the basement to do some bookkeeping. Twenty minutes later, they walked upstairs to find three tables completely overturned, as well as several chairs and a variety of dishes scattered about the floor. Not a sound had been heard by any of them while in the basement, and the four people were alone in a locked building.

In the 1970s, during the Whimples of Walnut Street era, the manager of the restaurant left one evening after arranging place settings for a large noon banquet the next day. When he returned the next morning, all the wine glasses had been reduced to piles of glass shards. Nothing else had been touched.

Rumor in Bloomington has it that Porticos was built over the foundation of another older house which was catastrophically destroyed in an engulfing fire. Perhaps this hinted-at past explains the next few odd occurrences. In the early 1980s, a passerby noticed smoke billowing out of the second story window of Porticos and called the Bloomington Fire Department. When the firemen arrived, they saw smoke but found no fire, nor any source of heat that could have caused the smoke in the first place. But there was more to the ghostly smouldering than just that one incident.

After serving a large banquet one evening, a waiter and waitress were sitting and chatting on a couch on the second floor at the foot of the attic stairs. Without warning, the waiter jumped off the couch and yelled, "Ouch! My back is on fire!" The waitress felt his back, and indeed it was burning hot. Several weeks later, a woman was checking her hair in the hall mirror when she saw reflected in the mirror smoke rising from that same couch. But when she whirled around, the smoke had vanished.

On another evening, those same audio monitors that had picked up the mysterious children playing detected the sounds of blaring radio broadcasts inside the building. But upon investigation, the owner found only two radios in the building, one of which was unplugged and the other which was turned off. No one had entered or left the building to either turn on or off the radios.

The attic also seems to be a place of unrest. A previous manager was terrified to go into the attic that was used for storage. Each time he opened the stairway door leading up into the gloom, a cold pressure would settle on his chest and he would be engulfed with feelings of impending doom. A previous owner of the building heard someone playing in the attic on what sounded like a rocking horse. He darted upstairs, but the attic was empty.

Mrs. Lewallen was working in her basement office one night when she heard footsteps upstairs, moving across the front room and into the kitchen. But by the time she got upstairs to investigate, she found no one else in the building and the doors securely locked.

Porticos is no longer open for business, at least to the living. Perhaps now that we pesky mortals are out of the way, the children can continue their play without interruption. Were they victims of an earlier fire that engulfed a previous home, or have they simply wandered in out of the dark, if you will, to join the frivolities that continue on to this day.[32]

The Lady-in-Grey

For more half a century, an apparition known simply as the Lady-in-Grey has wandered the halls of the Willard Library and has inspired many a ghost story over that time. No one is really sure who she might be, or where she may have come from, but it seems that she made her first publicly known appearance sometime in the 1930s. In those days, the janitor usually stayed late into the night at the building, normally staying until about ten p.m. After that point, he would go home for a bit, but would return around three a.m. to fire up the furnace.

During the Great Depression, it was not uncommon for hobos passing through the area to spend the night in the sheltered and warm basement of the library. But despite their presence, the staff slept soundly, knowing that the book collections were safe in a section locked and protected from the hobos. When the janitor would return to fire up the furnace, it was also his duty to make the rounds to check up on things, just to be safe.

One such night, the janitor whom we shall call George* was going through the doorway of the men's restroom, which was located in the safely locked section of the library, he suddenly and quite solidly bumped into a female figure. But by the time George could recover his wits and scan the area with his flashlight, she had disappeared.

From that night on, George saw her often, and not just in misty incoherence. Once he got a plain enough view to see that she wore a grey veil. Needless to say, these sightings disturbed George greatly. He grew afraid to come in at night, and eventually he quit his position because of the mysterious Lady-in-Grey.

Marie*, who served as the children's librarian for fifty years, saw the Lady-in-Grey many times and knew her best. She first saw the ghost in the mid 1950s. She and an assistant, Julia*, were often together when they saw her. Sometimes the figure was standing by the refrigerator in the old staff room. Other times the women arrived in the morning and hear scurrying, as if someone had just darted out of sight.

During remodeling of the childrens' room in 1980, Marie believed the Lady-in-Grey went for a time to live with her in her home, more than likely she thought to escape the confusion of the renovation. One day in Marie's house, her sister smelled a particular fragrance of perfume that had long been associated with the ghost. It made such an impression on her that she just had to bring it to Marie's attention. A week later they both smelled it again.

Not long after, the two ladies were sitting in the living room with their dog, when suddenly there was a noise in the kitchen that sounded like someone had opened a window and had knocked something over in the process. The dog went as far as the doorway to investigate, but refused to go into the kitchen itself. The sisters went in to find the clothes dryer running, the dampener ball tumbling around inside, and the timer set for ten minutes. Needless to say, neither Marie nor her sister had plans of doing the laundry that day.

On another evening, Marie actually saw the Lady-in-Grey pass from the dark dining room to the lighted living room. Marie could see the apparition's clothing so clearly that she could make out such details as long pleats in the back of the skirt. The dress, Marie noticed, was made from a woolen weave, but oddly, this time the ghost wore no veil. Marie called out to her sister, who came running just in time to see the figure turn into the living room and vanish.

But their house guest was short-lived. As soon as the renovation and remodeling was done at the library, the Lady-in-Grey returned to her old haunts, not to bother Marie or her sister again.

There was one other incident, about five years later, where Marie had another strange encounter with the unseen woman. Back in 1985, Marie and her sister were to give a preview of the Library's annual Easter Egg Tree to a group of women and children. A three-year-old boy wandered away from the group on the main floor and started up the stairs to the top floor. His mother tried to coax him back, but he said he didn't want to go in there "with that ghost."[33]

Working The Land

Talk to anyone who has grown up on a farm, and they will tell you without a doubt that farming is a harder job, and the farm is a more demanding workplace than any office building. Perhaps tired from their toils, these souls who "bought the farm" are resting for a spell on the land they once loved so dearly.

Back in 1972, Jennie's parents bought a 150-acre farm on the outskirts of Bloomington. Jennie's father had developed a romance with the concept of getting back to the land. But Jennie and her brother were not so entranced with the idea. After all, they were half an hour away from the city and their friends, and the isolation of a farm can be rather lonely.

From the time Jennie's family moved into the farm, old-timers told her parents of the unfortunate woman who had hanged herself in the woodshed next to the house. Jennie's cheerful pink bedroom looked down on that woodshed from the second story of the hundred-year-old farmhouse, and she rarely slept easily in that room. As a child, she always felt that someone was right behind her whenever she ascended the narrow stairs to the second floor. She had terrible nightmares about the grim reaper, shroud, scythe and grinning skull, coming for her, collecting his due. She refused to go downstairs at night, and when the electricity went off in the middle of a summer storm, she knew something dark and menacing waited for her in the shadows of the dark old house. She was absolutely terrified of whatever lay in wait in that pitch black country darkness.

Years passed, and Jennie decided to do a little research on the farm's history, to see what she could dig up. She learned that there really had been a woman who hanged herself there, a forty-year-old named Louisa Graves. The newspaper account from July 1894 said that the reasons were unknown; locals said she had been having an affair with a neighbor. Jennie's mother, who had lived in the farmhouse for only two years before her marriage ended in divorce, had no anxiety about the grounds whatsoever. She walked the property, even the woods, at night, and revelled in it. Jennie's father scoffs at the entire idea of the supernatural, and her brother is completely indifferent to the possibility that they had shared their farm with an unseen guest.

Nothing ever showed itself to Jennie over the years she lived there, but she was sure nevertheless that an invisible malevolent presence watched her every move. During her research on Louisa, Jennie also learned that further back in the farm's history, a onetime tenant farmer named Charles had gone insane while living there, and had killed himself. Rather than lonely Louisa, Jennie was sure that it was Charles who was sticking around, scaring the bejeesus out of her. Eventually, her parents sold the farm, and they moved away. Jennie never learned if something from the other side still wanders the farmhouse, something dark, lost in both the darkness of insanity and of unaccepted death.

Ida's Menace

Unfortunately, the story for Jennie, related in the previous tale, didn't end with her parents selling the farm. Her family moved into a tenant farm that also seemed to have the shadow of death draped lightly over the fields and buildings. It didn't take long, thanks to friendly neighbors and news clippings, to learn of another unhappy death, that of Mrs. Ida McConnell. Ida had been trampled to death by a team of horses as she fought to save her small grandson from the same fate. Her grandson survived, and still lives on a nearbyfarm. Ida may still be roaming the grounds, unhappy at the many years of life she lost, making everyone else there miserable at enjoying life themselves.

The first tenants of the house were a family with three girls, all close to Jennie's age. She had some wonderful times there as a child, but she would not spend the night in that house, though invited many times to sleep over. And as years went by, every couple who moved into the house was unhappily divorced before they moved out. Many tenants told of terrible nightmares during the first week of residence. On the occasions between tenants, when Jennie had the opportunity to be in the house alone, she felt all right about wandering around both upstairs and downstairs, but nothing in the world could have persuaded her to explore the attic. Something rotten waited there. Jennie, too, had strange and powerful nightmares centering on the upstairs bedroom that adjoins the attic.

She wanted so badly for someone to investigate, or validate, those feelings. No one else ever seemed to feel that anything was wrong. But one day three summers ago her husband helped out somewhat in that capacity. He was on a tractor, mowing in the field that was once the site of a schoolhouse, when he felt, or sensed, a presence that wanted him GONE. He continued his work, but not without looking over his shoulder every once in a while. He was a complete nonbeliever in the supernatural, but his feelings were altered after having that experience.

CHAPTER EIGHT

The Not-So-Happy Hunting Ground
Tales From and About the Natives

It is only arrogant presumption to believe that stories of ghosts and other mysterious occurrences began with the Europeans. There were hundreds of thriving cultures in the Midwest alone long before settlers pushed their way into the frontier that later became Indiana. Ghosts, spirits, mysterious realms and phantom animals have long been a part of the oral tradition of the Native Americans.

Take for example the realm of Galunlati. From the Cherokee tradition, Galunlati is the spirit realm that exists side-by-side with our own. And occasionally a mortal may stumble into, or go through rituals that allow passage into, this mysterious place. Other Native American cultures give us stories of the Weendigo, a voracious spirit of gluttony and excess that will devour any who get near it, and of Pauguk, the soul of a young man who killed his brother in lust for his brother's wife. Pauguk was doomed to become a spirit of bones who would never rest until a kind soul heard out his story and reassembled his bones into their proper order.

As settlers pushed into the frontier, they encountered both the stories and the people who created them. And there were bloody clashes. Native Americans and settlers alike fell beneath the gun or knife, many a time left where their bodies fell, never to receive burial, never to be brought home to their mourning families.

Indiana has a wealth of these stories handed down both from the diverse Native American cultures and from the European cultures that came after. A rich collection of legends, myths, and tales have sprung up around the rivers, hills and trees of Indiana. Tales of otherworldly spirit visitors go hand-in-hand with stories springing from the earliest settlement days, tales told around the campfires about Native Americans returning from the grave. Here are just a handful that have been passed down from generation to generation.

The Phantom Maiden

It seems that Indian apparitions have been quite common in Kosciusko County over the years. One such tale, one of the best known, speaks of a murdered Indian maiden and her flight to save her life. Her phantom is reported to most often appear just south of Leesburg near the road to Clunette. It seems that this young woman was somehow suspected of causing the death of Chief Monoquet. When she learned that she was suspected, she fled toward her home in Michigan. But before she could make it, she was overtaken and killed by two warriors from Chief Monoquet's tribe. The warriors left her body without preparation or ceremony as a reminder to all of the fate of traitors. But it seems that since burial of her body was never properly done, her spirit took to roaming the fields and woods near the scene of her death, forever tied to the land until she could be properly interred. To this day, many folks have caught a glimpse of the phantom maiden on her lonely trek to a home she may never reach.[34]

The Unseen River

Some great stories of the South Bend area were collected in a booklet made by the South Bend Community School Corporation. From that booklet, *The Spirit of South Bend*, we find this sad and frightening tale.

The St. Joseph River was known to the Native Americans of the area as Sauk-wauk-sil-buck, the name later shortened to Sau-was-see-be. This name refers to the Native American legends about the river and its spirit denizens. The legends tell that the St. Joseph River was believed to be one of a set of twin rivers. The one we are all familiar with is readily visible, flowing along above ground like any other river. Its twin, however, followed the same course, but deep underground, twisting through miles of subterranean passages. The Native Americans lived near this river and used it for fishing and transportation, and though they were well versed in the ways of the river, they always respected and feared it. The waters of the St. Joseph always ran colder than any other river in the area, and the Native Americans claimed that the spirit of the river each year claimed the lives of the two young people it admired most from the tribe.

Early autumn was the time for the river to seek its annual tribute. No one knew where the river spirit would strike; a friend's family one year, their own the next. Once, a set of lovely twin daughters were claimed by the voracious spirit. These two girls were known to be exceptional swimmers, as were most of the Potawatomi women. They were last seen in the vicinity of the river, and no trace of their bodies was ever found. Their drowning could only have been explained as the sacrifice to the river spirit, who hungrily took them down to the hidden twin of the river above.

You might think that since the spirit claimed twins that year, it might be sated for a bit. Yet a year later, the spirit of the St. Joseph struck again. Another tribe of Potawatomi had made their village along the river. The chief of this tribe had many children. He loved his children very much, and most of all he adored his young son. One day in early autumn, while the air was still warm, and the river water still bore the warmth of the summer now passing, the chief's little son wandered down to the river's shore. This innocent young Potawatomi boy began playing at the edge of the water, not directly in the stream itself. He had been warned many times to stay out of the main stream. One second he was there, the next instant, he was gone, vanished. No one saw what had happened, and his body was never found. His people searched for days, but to no avail. Secretly, they all knew they would never find the child. The river spirit had claimed another victim.

The old chief mourned the loss of his favorite son deeply and for a very long time. He would spend his days and nights sitting by the river where the little boy was last seen. At times he would wander the banks, calling his son's name. One cold winter night the tribe found the frozen body of their chief leaning against a tree near the river, still searching for his lost son.

Many years later, long after the river had changed its course, a school house was built on the very spot where the chief was found dead. The memory of the lost child lingers on, for residents of that school have seen the shadowy form of the Potawatomi chief roaming the building, searching even in death for his lost son.[35]

The Return of White Wolf

The story of "White Wolf" dates back far into the 154-year history of Lafayette, and was first reported in the *Evening Courier* in a two-part series on June 21 and 22, 1872.

William S. Lingle, then editor of the *Evening Courier*, had the privilege of being the dinner host for a distinguished group of gentlemen, including Judge B. K. Higginbotham of the county criminal court, a Professor Amos S. Dillington from London, and two men from eastern newspapers. Lingle's home was a charming house overlooking the Wabash Valley on what was then—and now—called Lingle Avenue.

In the course of the conversation, the five gentlemen discovered a mutual interest in the supernatural, whereupon Lingle told his guests of a supposedly haunted house. The house stood at the site of an abandoned brickyard, which was situated "at the head of North Street, extending eastward half a mile past the city limit." The one-and-one-half story building, its windows missing, had two ground floor rooms and no secret passages or closets.

The group of men decided to have some fun. The five drove by carriage out to the supposedly haunted house around 8:30 p.m. on the night of June 20, looked the house over carefully, and waited in silence inside from 9:00 until about 10:00 p.m.

At that hour an eerie blue-white light entered the cool chamber where the men watched. The light hovered like a cloud, then burned white and formed the image of a white wolf, which trotted and ran, slowing as though exhausted by a long run. It then raised its head and uttered a frightful howl.

Next the apparition began to transform into the shape of an indescribable creature which seemed to have the body of a large frog, jaws like an alligator, and a tail like a kangaroo. The creature floated almost motionless for about five minutes or so, when suddenly it changed into a cloud-like form which solidified into a powerful-looking Indian warrior, a tomahawk in one hand, a blazing torch in the other. The Indian then walked out into the open air and vanished towards the northeast.

The men were shaken by what they had just witnessed and returned to Lingle's home quickly. But Professor Dillington, reputed to possess a knowledge of magic, was determined to investigate. After quite a bit of cajoling, he convinced the others to return with him to the house. Dillington took with him a curious telescoping metal wand in a wooden case. When the group reached the house for the second time that night, he ushered them all inside, where he removed the wand from the case and with it drew on the dirt floor of the house a circle seven feet, seven inches in circumference, dividing it into 45 degree intervals and drawing in each section a series of mystical signs.

The Professor then set up in the middle of the circle on a small tripod a lamp made of several metals, and in it he burned a sick-smelling fluid that emitted a sickly green flame. Out of the flame and smoke there appeared the image of the Indian warrior they had seen previously, dressed in war costume.

Dillington calmly communicated with the Indian in an unintelligible language, the Indian replying in French-English with a halting dialect. The Indian informed the gentlemen that in life he had been known as White Wolf, and bore a tattoo on his right arm in the shape of the frog-like beast, a beast which ages before White Wolf claimed had abounded in western rivers.

White Wolf told of being buried in an old Indian cemetery on the Longlois reservation northeast of Lafayette, only to have his ashes stirred and disturbed by the shovels of the dwellers of the growing city. The disturbance of his gravesite was what was causing him to reappear.

The *Evening Courier* articles were the talk of the town for many months. Some time later, a resident of Linnwood, then a community of its own at the northeast edge of Lafayette, claimed to have a half-breed Indian employee who had spoken to White Wolf many times after the latter's death. White Wolf, the half-breed said, would never rest until a fence was built around the Spring Vale Cemetery, which opened in 1868.

But where exactly was the house containing White Wolf's spirit? In the 1872 description, the ground was situated half a mile east of the city limit on North Street, and extended past Barbee's Grove. The city limit in 1872 ended at about 18th Street. Barbee's Grove is the hilltop growth of trees known today as Murdock Park. Thus the abandoned brickyard and the haunted house evidently stood to the east of Murdock Park, possibly in the general vicinity of today's Sunnyside Junior High.

That fence around the Spring Vale Cemetery was never constructed, but the spirit of White Wolf seems to be at rest, for he has not been seen nor heard from for a little over a hundred years. Maybe he, in all his forms, has found his way to the Happy Hunting Ground at last.[36]

The Ghost of Black Rock

Apparently the *Evening Courier*, with their story of the ghost of White Wolf, had competition back in the late 1800s for reports of the supernatural. In August of 1890, the *Lafayette Morning Journal* reported an encounter between the ghost of an Indian chief who inhabited Black Rock, and an aspiring reporter writing under the name of 'Morning Glory.'

Black Rock is an interesting geological formation on private land twelve miles southwest of Lafayette, and has been the subject of poems, novels, and ghost stories for many years. The *Morn-*

ing Journal reported this story in two installments, and the narrative was so enjoyable I have included it here in its entirety:

About half way between Lafayette and Attica, on the line of the Wabash river, there rises above the shining waters a huge mass of rock, black, frowning and majestic. Its unpronounceable Indian name was changed to that of 'Black Rock' and such it has been called ever since the foot of the white man first pressed the fertile soil of the surrounding country.

Here it was that the red man of Ohio, Indiana, and Illinois met for council and treaty. On the high bank opposite was solemnly performed the "Sun Dance" and other religious ceremonies, and the gnarled old oaks still standing on the spot have doubtless been the silent witnesses of many a human sacrifice. The top of the rock is about 150 feet above the level of the surrounding country, and from time to time huge masses have become detached from the main body and fallen into the river.

These form a convenient landing place for the numerous curiosity hunters and sightseers who come in great number every summer to muse, speculate, carve their names upon the rock and depart with the baffled feeling caused by an unsolvable puzzle. The rock is seamed and worn by the storms of unnumbered winters and within are several caves where slimy serpents find a home. There is a tradition of rich treasure concealed in their cool recesses, but no one reaches for it for fear of the ghost that is its guard.

This spirit is often seen by fishing parties. A pale opalescent light flickered from the mouth of a cave overlooking the river and a skeleton form flits about its rugged entrance. This has been often seen but until last week no effort has ever been made to get a near view of the apparition.

Your correspondent with a party of friends was visiting a fishing camp at Secol's old trading post just below the rock and when night drew her dusky curtains over the landscape we set out in a boat to watch for the appearance of the ghost.

A faint moonlight shone upon the water and lent a weird look to the objects on the banks. The trees looked unnaturally tall and their shadows on the waters seemed like deep pits ready to swallow our little boat and all its occupants. A gay song was sung at starting but a hush soon fell upon the party, for argue as we will and protest our disbelief in spirits, ghosts and all things supernatural, the approach at night to a spot which they are said to frequent will cause an unusual length and frigidness about the spinal column. 'Tis a sad admission of weakness, but true, nevertheless.

Our little boat glided over the water, propelled by the strong strokes of an expert oarsman, and not a word was spoken. The only sounds that broke the stillness of night were the distant, dismal howl of a heartbroken dog, and occasionally the shrill unearthly cry of a screech owl from the deep shadows of the trees on the bank.

At last the rock was reached, and resting before it we looked anxiously for the strange light, half afraid that we would see, half afraid that we would not. We looked up until our necks ached; made ghastly attempts to be merry, until, tired of watching, we splashed our hands in the warm water and were about to float back to camp, when my companion, with white lips and staring eyes, whispered to me to look up.

I looked and sure enough at the mouth of the cave on an irregular pile of rocks there sat a skeleton form of huge proportions, bathed in the strangest light that ever shown on land or sea. Its chin rested on the palm of a large bony hand and with intense sad eyes it watched the rippling water.

Pulling to the landing was only the work of a moment, and heedless of the whispered entreaty not to go, I stepped upon the slippery rock and began my toilsome ascent.

"Won't you come too?" was asked of my companion when a firm foothold was reached, but my request was answered by a decided "No, but I'll try to stay here until you come back, if you ever do."

This was discouraging to me but I must not be laughed at down at the camp, so I went on. The way was rugged and steep and I could have made better headway, perhaps, if something less uncanny awaited me at its end, but I struggled on, looking up occasionally to see if he whom I sought was still musing.

At last I reached the level leading to the mouth of the cave and just then a stone loosened by my foot fell with a bound and a crash down the steep pathway. The advance of a half dozen steps and my ardent desire was gratified, for I stood in the presence of the celebrated "Ghost of Black Rock!"

He was evidently 'not at home' to visitors who threatened, and turned on me fiercely, and in a hollow voice that seemed to come from the ground said "Who are you, and what pup of Satan brings you here?"

"I beg your pardon sir. I intrude," I said in a trembling voice that sounded strangely unlike my own, "But I am a correspondent of the *Lafayette Journal* and I wish to interview you."

"Sure it's the *Journal*?" he asked suspiciously.

"Quite sure," I answered him. Then he made me a stately bow and brushing the dust from a rock opposite him, politely requested me to be seated. I obeyed, for I was feeling very weak about the knees, and then he sank back upon his rock with a deep sigh, and resumed his former attitude.

"Venerable spook," I began, "how long have you haunted this rock?"

"Not long," he answered. "Only about 150 years, though I have known this country for ages. I lived here in the flesh in the year 900 and was chief."

Some pebbly tears fell from his eyes and he continued, "This country isn't what it was in those days. This insignificant stream at our feet was a mighty river, spreading from bluff to bluff and carried on its

bosom such fleets of canoes filled with my painted people, that I would fain turn backward the march of time and see it once again."

"Those were stirring times and 'tis hard for one who lived in them to be a mere shade, condemned to sit idle year after year, with no companions but these cold serpents and insensible rocks. The serpents do not fear me and I would not harm them if I could."

"The meanest creature of the Great Spirit has the same right to life that you have, and beware how you take it if you would be happy hereafter. I slaughtered ruthlessly anything that stood in my way, man or beast, and I am being punished for it. I was finally killed myself in a battle over yonder with poisoned arrows, and I discovered that this dying is no fun."

"The tribes assembled and they buried my body with ceremonies befitting a great chief. I watched it all poised in the air, a free spirit, and they gave me a send-off that was very gratifying to my pride. They danced and feasted for three days, and the quantity of maize and raw dog that was consumed was astonishing."

"The chief who took my place was an irrepressible customer with whom I would have had trouble if I had lived. He always wanted to run things and he does yet. He is reincarnated now and is one of the most prominent men in your government today. If I only had a body I would show him a trick or two. He used to steal ponies and now he steals thunder. The last I heard of him he had grabbed another man's cards and was playing his hand out."

"Have you never left the earth?" I asked.

"Yes, I have been to the Happy Hunting Grounds, but I don't like it. The game is too tame so I left it and went below for a change. Satan treats me well and this night I must return to his kingdom to look after things while he attends camp meeting."

"This rock is more like my home than any place I find, for here my happiest days were passed. On its top I placed the crown of authority upon my head, and touched it to the brow of Laska, my eagle-eyed bride. She rode beside me in battle and when I fell, she came here and in a frenzy of grief threw herself into the raging torrents below. Her spirit is now in Devachan but it will soon return to earth and then . . ."

"What will happen?" I asked.

"We will be reunited!" he replied with the happiest smile I ever saw. "I have waited for a thousand years, but I shall be rewarded, dearest Laska, sister of the stars and the night wind, my soul's mate!"

He stretched up his arms toward the sky in ecstasy, but the sudden motion alarmed me, and I was half way down the rock before I knew what I was doing.

"What? Are you going?" he called after me.

"Yes," I answered, "And please excuse the manner of it; many thanks for your kindness."

"Come back one year from tonight and I will tell you the secret of the rock," he said, then vanished from sight.[37]

There is no indication that the intrepid reporter ever ventured back one year later to continue his discourse with the Ghost of Black Rock. No one ever learned what the secrets were that the ghost was hiding. And for all we know, he waits there still for the return of his beloved Laska, serving as guardian of the secrets possessed by Black Rock, secrets that still await the adventurous. But if you *do* go adventuring one dark evening along the river and happen to encounter the grisly skeleton alone in the gloom, you might want to make sure you have your press pass along. I hear he's particular to exclusive interviews.

The Lost Brave

Back in the early settlement days of South Bend, when the land was still wild and mostly untamed, there lived a solitary woman by the name of Polly Pratt. Her cabin sat on a piece of land that would one day become what is now known as Chapin Park. It seems that Polly was a wicked, mean-spirited woman who was neither trusted nor ever befriended by any of the other settlers in the little town of South Bend. That suited Polly just fine. She did not consider herself a member of the newly-formed country. Polly was a French woman, and saw herself as a colonist for France. She was not at all fond of any of the American settlers in the town. In fact, the only people she ever welcomed on her land were the Indians.

These Indians would come to town with their hard-won pelts to trade for goods and food stuffs. But unfortunately, thanks to the wiles of unscrupulous white traders, they would more often than not come away with several bottles of liquor instead. And with the liquor in hand, they would gather on Polly Pratt's land to spend a joyous time drinking and planning how they would kill all the white settlers in the town, with the exception, of course, being Polly herself.

As one especially inebriating evening wore on, plans of their fantastic massacre become more riotous. In fact, in became more than plans. The intoxicated Indians jumped up, and while wildly dancing about, began demonstrating in quite graphic pantomime, how they would kill all the white men. And in the midst of the drunken fracas, a young Indian brave was accidentally killed.

Needless to say, the life went out of the party after that. The Indians started out for home that very night, rather than stay another minute where one of their own comrades had been slain by their own excess. After that night, the Indians never returned to Polly's land again. And no one seems exactly sure what ever became of Polly. But locals do say the spirit of the young Indian brave still hovers in the old trees of Chapin Park, looking for his friends with eternal longing, hoping for his own opportunity to return with them to his Indian village.[38]

CHAPTER NINE

LIONS, TIGERS AND BIGFOOT, OH MY!
Mysterious Animals and Unexplained Beasts

Remember when you were little, when monsters lurked under your bed or in your closet? Back then, I'm sure you wouldn't have doubted for a moment that creatures both strange and terrifying lurked in the shadows of the not-so-distant woods. But for some reason, as we grow older we become convinced that such notions are childish, foolish rampagings of an overactive imagination.

There have been reports of strange beasts and mystical animals in the hills of Indiana that go back hundreds of years. From mysterious water monsters to amorphous flying beasts to bigfoot-like apparitions, the stories simply abound. They come from sources too diverse and respectable to simply brush off as publicity stunts or late night indulgences in other more potable "spirits." But what exactly have these people seen over the years? Are they truly hidden creatures only occasionally glimpsed? Are they ghosts? Or, are they something even more strange—ghosts of the mind?

Tibetan monks have long held a belief in a phenomena called a *tulpa*. In short, a *tulpa* is a phantom form generated by mental concentration or thought. They believe that thoughts have weight and reality, and that when given enough energy, they can manifest themselves in visible forms. But these *tulpas* need not be the result of one singular conscious thought. They can arise spontaneously as archetypes which then take on real form. Perhaps that is why sightings of bigfoot-like creatures, no matter where they come from, all bear a striking similarity.

Noted anthropologist and explorer Alexandra David-Neel (1868-1969) first described the phenomena of the *tulpa* in her

1931 book, *With Mystics and Magicians in Tibet*. French traveler and Tibetan scholar, David-Neel, was the first European woman ever to enter the forbidden city of Lhasa in Tibet.[39] There she studied for fourteen years and herself achieved the rank of Lama. In her book, she wrote of her successful attempt to create a *tulpa*. For months she concentrated on the image of a fat jolly jovial monk. She pictured his clothes, his physical appearance, his personality. And after six months, the monk appeared. He was so real in appearance that he was regarded as a regular member of David-Neel's expedition team.

But somehow, her experiment got out of hand. The formerly rotund monk took on a gaunt hollow appearance. And where he was once friendly, he became sly and malignant, always leering at those around him. He became so destructive that David-Neel was forced to dispel him, again after many months of concentration. She was never sure how the *tulpa* took on its own personality and will, but it unnerved her greatly. There is no record of her ever attempting to create a *tulpa* again.

Could this explanation be the reason for these mysterious appearances all around the Hoosier state? Could these strange beasts be *tulpas*, actual physical manifestations of thought? Or are they something more unexplainable, relics of a distant age? I leave the judgement up to you.

The Kosciusko Serpent

Scotland is not the only locale that can lay claim to beastly water monsters. Reports come from all over the world, including right here in North America, of isolated sightings especially around deep-water lakes, of long snakelike creatures that rise from the depths momentarily, look about and then dive out of sight, leaving the witness rattled and confused. Scientists remain baffled as to what people are seeing. Some speculate that, just as the coelacanth, a prehistoric fish long thought extinct until recently, survived for millions of years

Lake Manitou, home of the Manitou Monster

unknown to man, perhaps small isolated families of plesiosaurs, an ancient water predator with a long snakelike neck and flippers, may be responsible for all these sightings. And although the most famous photograph of "Nessie" was recently, upon the deathbed of the perpetrator, discovered to be a hoax, there remains hundreds of other glimpses of these strange creatures from around the world.

Lake Champlain is one of North America's most famous spots, home to "Champ," an unknown beast that lurks in the depths of the lake. But you needn't travel that far north for thrills; just go to Northern Indiana!

Charlotte Seigfried sent me a little tidbit from her own family's past. Her grandparents, while boating on day out on Center Lake in Kosciusko County, spotted what they thought was an overturned boat that had capsized. Of course the first thought to enter their minds was to see if anyone required assistance. But as they approached to offer what help they could, the "overturned boat" suddenly reared up and came to life. It splashed about quite violently, then with a great twist dove and disappeared into the depths of the lake. Whatever the creature was, it didn't stay still long enough for the couple to get a good look at it. But if it had been the size of an overturned boat, it would have been quite some creature.

Over the years, there have been countless sightings of large creatures in Kosciusko County's one hundred plus lakes. Such sightings continue to this day, especially in Center Lake and Pike Lake.[40]

The Manitou Monster

There have been reports for years of the Lake Manitou serpent, another creature that bears a striking resemblance to the Center Lake serpent. The Potawatomi Indians have long known of the existence of something strange in Lake Manitou. They tell of a great flood that covered the land that was caused by the thrashing about of a huge dying creature, a "manitou" or spirit. The creature twisted around and splashed until a wall of water rose up and flooded the world. Lake Manitou supposedly was connected to the Great Lakes by an underground passage, and as the flood rose, torrents of water poured through this underground passage to flood the Potawatomi lands.

John Lindsay, the first blacksmith in the area, was the first white man in recorded history to see the monster. His family holds another first as well. Lindsay's wife is honored by a grave marker in front of the Fulton County Historical Society Museum as the first white woman to die in that county. John described the monster: "The head being about three feet across the frontal bone and having something of the contour of a beef's head, but the neck tapering and having the character of the serpent; color dingy with large yellow spots." Settlers didn't take John too seriously at first, not until a group of fishermen ran practically right into the beast. In July of 1838, several more men saw the monster and quickly rowed to shore. They claimed it was sixty feet long.

There was a great deal of discussion in Logansport about forming an expedition to make an attempt to capture the monster, though nothing like that seems to have materialized. No more sightings that we know of were reported until May 26, 1849, when the *Logansport Journal* ran a headline, "The Devil Caught at Last." A huge buffalo carp was caught, weighing several hundred pounds. The head, which weighed thirty pounds, was taken to Logansport. But although a large fish was indeed caught, it in no way matched the description given by John Lindsay or the other men in 1838.

Could Lindsay and his compatriots have seen a plesiosaur? The idea is intriguing to say the least. If the Potawatomi are correct, and there does indeed exist an underground passage between Lake Manitou and the Great Lakes, then any manner of creature could travel back and forth from open sea to inland Indiana lake at a whim. And Lindsay's description of the head of the creature matches quite well what the head of a plesiosaur would look like.

But in any event, the Lake Manitou monster has not been seen for many years. Perhaps the creature died, or its underground passage collapsed. But a similar creature was sighted in Kings Lake in 1894. This lake too is reputed to be very deep, and filled with secret passages and underwater caves. Perhaps the fabled monster went there by means of an underground river.[41]

The Demon in the Deep

The Blue Hole along the Wabash River is a landmark that has become part of Vigo County's culture. The Blue Hole was a tough part of Indiana back in the early days of settlement and river trade. And although it may not look like much now, the Blue Hole has seen a lot of history. Residents near the Hole used to claim that a demon lived at the bottom of the Hole, and would from time to time rise to the surface and occasionally pull those unlucky enough to be on the surface of the Blue Hole down into the inky depths.

The method of the Demon's assault varies from victim to victim. Sometimes swimmers feel a tug on their legs, then another, and another. The unfortunate soul makes a desperate attempt to swim to safety, until he or she is pulled under for the final time, taken down forever into the realm of the Demon.

Other times, the Demon reaches out and takes it victims much more ruthlessly. In one hideous attack, a massive wave caused by the Demon itself is said to have swept across the road and carried away a school bus filled with children. Needless to say, there is absolutely no record of this ever happening. Yet there are those who insist that the tragedy was real, and that rather than admit to the existence of the Demon, the local authorities covered up the entire episode.

During the 20s and 30s, speakeasies and brothels flourished in the area of the Blue Hole. Moonshiners and gamblers took advantage of the Hole's reputation and used it as a dumping ground for the bodies of their hapless victims. The bodies would be trussed up, weighted with lead or stones, and dumped down into the depth of the Hole.

Divers in 1971 found the supposed bottom of the Blue Hole, some twenty-two feet from the surface. But again there are always the staunch few who insist that the Hole goes deeper than that. The stories persist of limitless depths and of the Demon waiting in some watery pit of hell. After all, they claim, how do we know that the divers found the real bottom, and not just some clever illusion or trick arranged by the demon who wants us to *think* it's safe . . . until it's ready to strike again.[42]

The Parke County Monster

During the summer of 1972, Putnam, Parke, and Montgomery counties were visited by what some believed to be a cousin of the infamous Bigfoot. On September 20, 1972, the Parke County Sheriff's Department issued a warning about a monster that was ten feet tall and furry. The monster sparked interest from the F.B.I., who offered to help search for the creature.

The Parke County monster was described as being similar to the monster that had been seen around Roachdale and the Ladoga area of Montgomery County, and was known to kill chickens, dogs, and pigs. These monsters stirred up much interest in the area, provoking "monster hunts" and leading to quite a mystery for area residents. The monster in the Crawfordsville area sparked such interest that it was reported in Jerome Clark's book, *Unexplained*.

Later in the year, some of the occurrences were blamed on the pranks of local youths, but no evidence was found to substantiate that claim. The native people of that area have, for hundreds of years, viewed the woods around Montgomery and Parke counties with respect, awe, and even a little dread. They had always felt that there were mysterious aspects to those woods. Although quite a bit of the forest in those counties has been converted into farmland since those early days, there still remains parcels of the original old growth forests preserved in Shades and Turkey Run State Parks and in the surrounding lands that few, if any, have completely traversed. To this day, no one really knows what lurks deep in the old growth forests of west central Indiana.[43]

The Crawfordsville Monster

In the fall of 1891, two men, Marshall McIntyre and Bill Grant, who were working in the middle of the night at a local ice house, sensed a presence. They described it as a feeling of "awe and dread." The two men looked toward the night sky and viewed "a horrible apparition approaching from the west." They reported it was about three to four hundred feet in the air and was "eighteen feet long and eight feet wide." The creature was moving through the air by means of "side fins" and was pure white with a "flaming red eye." The beast was "wheezing" and moaning as if in great pain. It hovered directly over a house and then flew off to the east, but after reaching the Crawfordsville city limits turned back to hover once more in nearly the same location.

The first viewing took place on September 5, 1891 and was explained at first as the visions of two men who had consumed far too many spirits themselves. However, on September 7, 1891, more witnesses stepped forward to back up their story. including Reverend G. W. Switzer of the Methodist Church and his wife. Reverend Switzer stated that "it was about sixteen feet long and eight feet wide" and that it resembled a mass of floating drapery. The reverend and his wife watched the thing, which he said moved like a "serpent," rise up and down, circling the town until he and his wife became tired and went back inside their house.

No one is sure what the Crawfordsville sighting was. St. Elmo's Fire? A conglomeration of spirits dancing through the night? Or some strange beast let loose from the deep forests to the west of Crawfordsville, rising up out of the darkness from the Shades of Death itself.[44]

The Devil Dog

Many ghostly animals have been spotted in Koscuisko County, such as mysterious disappearing black panthers and the Churubusco turtle. Daniel*, a young man who grew up and still lives in that area, related this story to me one evening. In his own words, this chilling tale of the unexplained unfolds:

> In the late winter of 1992, I was driving home with my friend near Pike Lake. It was quite late, somewhere around one-thirty in the morning, and the weather was very clear. Although it had been bitterly cold, no snow had fallen yet that season. We were making general conversation, talking about music, girlfriends, all the typical things that eighteen-year-olds talk about. And although I was paying attention to my driving, we both were not paying too much attention to anything else, being caught up in our discussions. The area we were driving through is somewhat wooded. It wasn't out-and-out farm

country, but then again, it was rural enough that we didn't see any lights or houses about.

We were driving through a particularly heavily wooded area, when suddenly up ahead at an intersection, a LARGE dog came into the light of our headlights. It stood at least four foot high, and was covered with completely black fur. Its bright white eyes and large white teeth were clearly visible in the cold moonlight. We had been in mid-conversation when we both first caught sight of the beast, but we each fell silent with terror as I stopped the car and watched the thing in the middle of the road. It was watching us as well!

The creature remained in the middle of the intersection, not budging an inch. Finally we had had enough, and I stepped on the accelerator, lurched the car forward, and swerved around the beast. It remained stock still as we sped past, just watching us intently as we dodged to miss hitting it.

I got a good look at whatever it was as we flew by, and it did not look natural. It was much too big, and too strange looking, to be a dog, and a wolf would have been unheard of in Indiana. Needless to say, it scared me quite a bit.

After passing it, I turned to my friend and asked him if he truly saw the same thing that I just saw. He said that he had, and once we had let our hearts calm down a bit, I turned the car around to try to get a better look at the creature. We had only gone maybe seventy-five feet past the intersection, but in the time it took me to turn around (maybe all of thirty seconds), it had vanished, leaving only an open and empty country road intersection. It was at that point that I chose to get the hell out of there.

My friend and I talked about it that night . . . each of us pretty spooked. Just seeing it gave my the strangest feeling. I could not dismiss it as a regular large dog—it was so different than that.

It wasn't until I ran into an old friend from school and told her my story of that night did my feelings change about what I saw. I told her what I had seen, and she was thrilled. For she had seen the same creature many years ago when she was a child. She told me that every once in a while over the past hundred years or so, travelers will claim they see this black devil-dog off the roadways around Koscuisko County. I just never want to see it again.

A Hoosier Bigfoot?

An acquaintance of mine, Tom*, was quite reluctant to tell this story, as he is a man involved with local politics and what he described happened to a member of his family. He was afraid that people would think a strain of lunacy might have been passed down to him and doubt his judgement.

Tom described an evening back around 1910 or 1911. Three men, relatives all, were working the family farm near Moore's Hill. It had been a long summer's day of productive work, and the men relaxed for the first time that day as cool evening breezes touched the hilltops.

As one of the men looked about, admiring the day's work, he was startled and more than a little frightened to see a large man-shaped figure emerge from the adjoining woods next to their lawn. He slapped his companions in the arm to get their attention, and all three stared slack-jawed as the creature ran out of the woods and loped across the grass to disappear into the trees on the opposite side of the lawn, the only sound the crunch of the creature's running footfalls. One of the men later described to Tom a creature at least seven feet tall, very large, bent over, and covered in long black hair. It was a singular incident, for the creature was never seen again.

CHAPTER TEN

NOT-QUITE-LIVING HISTORY
The Culbertson Mansion State Historic Site

The Culbertson Mansion sits stoically in New Albany, an elderly and stately relic from an age gone by. With its hand-painted ceilings, carved rosewood staircase, marble fireplaces, and crystal chandeliers, the Culbertson Mansion reflects the affluence of a man once considered to be the wealthiest in Indiana. In 1867, William S. Culbertson spent just about $120,000 to build his grand home in New Albany, which was then the largest city in Indiana. The three-story Second Empire mansion encompasses over 20,000 square feet and is made up of twenty-five rooms.

To say the least, Culbertson was enormously rich. Starting in the dry goods business, he later invested his money in new ventures. These investments included purchasing managing stock in the Kentucky-Indiana Railroad Bridge Company and establishing his own utility company in 1854. When he died in 1892, he had achieved a net worth of 3.5 million dollars. Just imagine his wealth compared to today's values!

Built from 1867 to 1869, the mansion is decked in complete opulence, fitted with high, arched windows, circular turret, intricately carved privacy porches and mouldings. Acquired by the State of Indiana in 1976 from the Historic New Albany organization, it is now part of the State Historic Site program, where it is run as a museum and historical interpretation center.

As you enter the grand front hall, with the portraits of William and Cornelia Culbertson staring resolutely at all visitors, it is almost impossible to imagine the undercurrents of something unseen that seem to circulate more efficiently than the furnace air through the restored rooms and hallways.

In 1977, Joellen Bye, Historic Interpreter, came to be part of the staff at the mansion. Almost immediately, she began noticing more than history still living about her. She would sense a presence on the third floor while vacuuming, usually while her back was to the open door. She would turn around to see who was there, but of course, no one would be found.

There was also the continual sensing of a presence of "some-one" in the mansion by various other staff persons. Slowly, the presence was first sensed on the third floor. Later on the second, moving over a period of a few years. Strange happen-ings would continue in whatever floor the presence happened to be in, thus enabling the staff to track the progress of the presence as it moved down the house.

Whatever the presence was, it seemed to have a penchant for pulling pranks involving the vacuum cleaner. One day, Joellen was vacuuming the ballroom on the third floor and at noon when it was time for lunch she turned off the vacuum cleaner and walked the length of the room, about thirty-five feet away. Suddenly, the vacuum cleaner turned itself back on, as if wanting Joellen to continue with her duties.

One other morning Joellen was vacuuming the front hall carpet on the first floor. She went directly into the formal par-lor to vacuum a small area rug. About a minute later, she came back into the front hall, where she found pieces of dried flow-ers scattered all over the hall carpet. There was a dried ar-rangement sitting on the hall tree but it was undisturbed and intact. The carpet however, which had just been vacuumed, looked like someone had picked the flowers up, held them upside down and shook them as hard as they could.

The third floor seems to have a flurry of activity linked to it. It houses the children's bedrooms and a large ballroom which runs the entire width of the mansion. It is not hard to imagine jewel-bedecked ladies and elegant powerful men danc-ing gaily in through the warm spring night across the wooden inlaid floor. This floor has never been completely restored and was closed off in 1899 by the McDonald family when they pur-chased the home from the Culbertsons. Much later in history, from 1946 through the 1950s, the American Legion made some use of the ballroom for their pool hall. After that period, when

Historic New Albany acquired the house, it was only used as storage.

When the Department of Natural Resources incorporated the mansion as a State Historic Site, the condition of the entire third floor was very bad. Louis Jensen and Bob Slider spent months cleaning it out, shoveling out hundreds of pigeon skeletons and piles of bird droppings, trash, and various debris, such as old light fixtures. By the time Joellen came to work for the museum in 1977, the third floor was empty of all trash but was not clean. When she first vacuumed the ballroom floor, the filter in the vacuum cleaner had to be changed seven times. But as time and cleaning continued, she got down to three changes, then two, then finally one. At last the third floor was clean and could be vacuumed easily on one filter.

After dealing with the frustrating vacuum cleaner disturbances, Joellen was finally rewarded with what may have been a glimpse of who, or what, was making all the fuss. In December of 1984, Joellen was standing at the bottom of the front staircase in the first floor hall. She happened to glance upwards through the staircase towards the third floor and there she saw an elderly woman looking down at her. The woman, her gray hair done up in a bun, was leaning slightly over the bannister, looking intently down on Joellen. But when Joellen blinked her eyes a few times and looked again, the woman was gone.

Joellen saw the gray-haired woman again, nine months after the apparition's first appearance. It happened between 8:05 and 8:15 a.m., as Joellen was going through the house to open shutters. As she was entering the master bedroom from the front hall on the second floor, she saw the back side of the woman going out of the master bedroom through the west door into the servant's staircase and making a left. Joellen immediately went after her but the woman was gone. It seemed as if Joellen had "caught" her and she was in a hurry to get out of sight. No one else was in the house at the time. The gray-haired woman was wearing a long medium-gray dress with long sleeves.

In September of 1985, Dr. Tom Greco, a parapsychologist from the University of Louisville, on invitation from Linda Miller, a volunteer at the museum, went to visit the mansion. Lisa Higbee, then curator, was reluctant to allow Dr. Greco to visit, on the chance that he might stir something up. She resided in renovated servant's quarters, remodeled around 1980. After all, she was the one who had to live there, and the last thing she wanted was to have to deal with things that go bump in the night. But after about six months, she relented and allowed Dr. Greco to visit.

As he entered the home from the front door, Dr. Greco saw an elderly lady on the master staircase right at the turn near the coffin niche. (For those who are morbidly curious, many older homes were designed with "coffin niches," or recessed cubicles in the walls near staircases or other tight turns and corners. Since the majority of people died at home in those days, and were subsequently "laid out" in their homes, many builders would design these niches to allow the coffins an easier time around corners.) When Dr. Greco noticed the woman, she turned to go on up the stairs to the second floor as if to say, "Don't bother down there, come on up here." After introductions, Dr. Greco went to the dining room and then came back out asking the staff not to tell him anything about the home or the family. He also informed them that he preferred to go through the mansion without the benefit of electric lights.

While he was in the dining room, he sensed that a "presence" in the home wanted that room to be renovated. When questioned further on this he said it wasn't so much structural as artistic renovation, as if the family was embarrassed of the way the room looked. As he progressed into the formal parlor, the informal parlor, and the servant's quarters, he drew a blank, nothing. These rooms seemed untouched by the entity's presence.

He proceeded up to the second floor, and felt nothing in the office there. But, when he walked into the main hall to go into the twin bedroom, he was taken aback, and hesitated before continuing. He later said that he became short of breath and had to leave the room for a short while. The overwhelming feeling he got from the twin bedroom was that of death. After he toured the rest of the second floor he returned to this room, and sitting upon a borrowed office chair, related his feelings to Lisa: feelings of death, sickness, and of a woman who died therein.

The private parlor was also alive with emotion. Dr. Greco felt sickness, and conflicts over the Civil War. He said that there were many problems in the house and that it wasn't a happy one, and that many arguments took place in that room.

In the master bedroom he said he felt an elderly lady dying. He also sensed some fighting or bickering in the room, almost as if in whispers.

After he completed the second floor, the staff pointed out the stairs to the third floor. Although Dr. Greco didn't really want to go up there, he forced himself. He sensed nothing in the majority of the third floor, in the hall or ballroom. But in the north children's bedroom however he could see a dark-headed boy and a blond girl. They glanced at him as he entered, and slowly faded from his sight.

Dr. Greco left the room quickly and walked into the south children's bedroom. At first he felt nothing until he walked over to the doorway leading down into the back servant's stairway. He did not particularly want to go down there either. He sensed a tall man having to bend or stoop to avoid hitting the ceiling that curves down in this area. Not staying long in the servant's bedroom, he said that he couldn't explain the sensation he got from the stairway area at first. But as he thought about it, he later described it as an area of punishment, and a strong feeling of confinement.

What Dr. Greco did not know was that the Culbertson's were extremely strict disciplinarians, and that Eliza Culbertson would lock the children away in a "punishment closet" located in the hallway between the main residence and the servants' quarters. This closet is an ominous contraption made of latticework, where many a time a recalcitrant child would be locked away for hours until they learned the error of their ways.

The 'punishment closet' in the Culbertson mansion

After spending some time in that area, Dr. Greco commented that the Culbertson's were stricter that anyone had imagined. He strongly advised the staff not to spend extended periods of time on the third floor or near the punishment closet, explaining that if an area or a particular room has strong emotions, then those emotions can be transferred to people as they work in and about the affected area. Dr. Greco said also that "they" want the front half of the home taken care of, giving

Lisa the impression that "they" want the staff to either restore/renovate that section or close it off to the public.

The basement of the mansion contains the main kitchen, where servants would prepare the meals and send them up through the house by means of a dumbwaiter, as well as the coal bin, and a large open area for laundry and various sundry chores. As Dr. Greco toured the basement, he asked Lisa if President Lincoln had ever visited the home, as he was getting an image of a man who looked startlingly like the former President. Lisa replied that no, Lincoln had never been there, but that William Culbertson had looked remarkably like Abraham Lincoln. Dr. Greco also picked up the feeling of Quaker religious services in the basement, and the feelings of school lessons going on.

What really *is* known about the Culbertsons, and their mysterious mansion? Well, the master bedroom where Dr. Greco sensed the presence of an elderly woman dying was the bedroom of Mr. and Mrs. Culbertson. But during one part of their life in the house, an elderly aunt lived with them for a time while she was being cared for in her last days of life. She spent her final days in the master bedroom, and eventually died there. And as far as death in the twin bedroom, William, Cornelia, and Walter Culbertson all died in that section of the house.

The Culbertson Mansion could not have been a pleasant place to abide in during the early years of its history. Five of Eliza Culbertson's brothers fought for the Confederacy during the Civil War, and five fought for the Union. We can no doubt imagine the heated discussions this family rift would have caused, and the arguments it might have spurred.

Dr. Greco also picked up whispered arguments or bickering in the master bedroom. It is known that William Culbertson and some of his children were extremely opinionated. At William's death, there was an argument over his daughter Blanche's choice of a beau, as her father had forbade her from marrying a Frenchman. Anne, his other daughter, wanted to

The bed where Cornelia Culbertson died.

move out of the house before she was married, and his son Charlie was an alcoholic. Small wonder there were many whispered arguments going on behind closed doors.

In October of 1985, the staff decided to open up the mansion as a "haunted house" for the Jaycee's Annual Spook Run. The first floor was decorated with props and cobwebs as well as the second floor front hall and the entire third floor. Joellen made two ghosts out of white sheets that were attached to pulleys. Both ghosts worked at the same time, being on the same line. As one flew down the third floor hall from the front window to the staircase, the other one was going down through the main staircase dropping from the third floor to the first floor, terrifying visitors.

On one of the tapes used for sound effects, there was found one night a woman's crying embedding in the prerecorded tracks of the tape, a woman crying repeatedly. The crying had not been on the tape before and it was not heard on the tape after that one night. On another night, at about 10:30 p.m., the lights in the southwest bedroom, and back hallway of the third floor went out. The staff changed the bulbs and checked the circuit breakers, but to no avail. Suddenly at 11:30 p.m., the lights came back on by themselves.

At the end of the first night of haunted house duty, after the last visitor had left the premises, Lisa, Diedra, Joellen, and Linda, were sitting on the floor of the first floor front hallway. They were exhausted from a hard night's work keeping the haunted house running smoothly, and they sat quietly talking amongst themselves, when suddenly there were the sounds of footsteps. It was coming from the third floor, a woman's shoes echoing off the wooden floors. They immediately stopped talking and listened; one step, two, three, four, five, six, seven, eight steps and it stopped. They all sat there looking at each other saying, "I heard that, did you hear that? We heard that didn't we?" It was the first time a group experience had ever happened in the mansion. It was at that point that occurrences picked up and the "happenings" became more and more frequent, louder, and more evident to everyone.

On another night during the haunted house stint, in the last weekend of October, Lisa Higbee invited the staff to spend the night in the mansion due to the late hours everyone had been working in order to make the haunted house such a suc-cess. Joellen went to go to sleep in the large bed in the twin bedroom. There were no lights in this room so a kerosene lamp was used for illumination. Shortly after she got into bed, a very foul odor like the stench of dead fish, settled down around her and upon the bed. After five minutes, the smell still had not dissipated, and was actually getting stronger. Joellen decided that there was no way she could get any sleep with that horrible smell around her all night. Not wanting to be branded a "chicken," she decided to try something. She spoke to the "smell" and told it to go away, get out, and leave her alone. Within one minute, the smell was gone completely and Joellen spent the rest of the night undisturbed.

The next morning, other staff members got up talking and complaining about the noises all night long. The sounds had been so loud that neither Lisa nor Diedra had been able to catch more than a few minutes sleep here and there. They both heard loud bangings and doors slamming on the third floor above them. Remarkably, Joellen, who had been just across the hall from them, had heard nothing during the entire night.

The Great Balloon Heist

The Sunnyside Tourism Bureau held a small wine and cheese reception late one afternoon at the Culbertson Man-sion for a group of tour bus drivers. Someone had decorated with helium-filled balloons and the group arrived around 4:15 p.m. Shortly after 5:00 p.m. a woman leaving asked to take some balloons with her. But before she got to the front door, she lost her grip on the balloons and they floated up to the fifteen-foot-high ceiling. The five balloons were all attached together with lengths of ribbon. Since the staff would have to bring in the tallest ladder to reach them, and due to the late hour, they decided to leave them until morning, knowing that the balloons could go nowhere.

Well, ghosts must like balloons as much as people do. For around 2:30 a.m. . . . . Joellen got a call from the alarm company, indicating that there was movement in the mansion and that they couldn't reach Lisa Higbee in the servant's quarters by phone. Joellen drove to the mansion and found Lisa sleeping in her bedroom. For some odd reason, her telephone simply refused to ring.

Both Joellen and Lisa decided it must have been the balloons that triggered the alarm, but when they went to retrieve them, they were gone. Thinking that they must have drifted off over to the staircase and floated on up, Lisa and Joellen went in search of the wayward decorations. They went first to the third floor, the highest point, but the balloons were not there. Joellen decided to look on the second floor, but they were not in the hallway. Joellen began looking in the other rooms on the second floor. When she got to the north door to the twin bedrooms she saw the balloons, or rather the shadow of the balloons as it was very dark in the bedroom with only the hall light barely filtering into the chamber. What she found was even stranger than the disappearance of the balloons themselves.

There they were, all five balloons, wrapped around a dress that had been placed on display, the dress of Anne Culbertson. What was most unusual was the path the balloons had to take to get where they were now resting. They travelled approximately fifteen feet along the first floor ceiling over to the front staircase. Now, instead of going straight up, they would have had to stop at the second floor and travel thirty feet down the second floor hallway. Then the balloons would have had to go through the north bedroom door, which is only ten feet high (so the balloons lowered themselves five feet to make it through), cross over another fifteen feet to the wardrobe where the dress was on display, and then tangle themselves around the sleeves of Anne Culbertson's dress.

Other occurrences have been experienced in the mansion, though none quite so dramatic as the balloon incident. The rich aroma of pipe tobacco has been smelled in the formal parlor on several occasions. People have heard a man's voice in the front hall. In the back servants' stairs, something bangs up against the walls, rattling the wood, as if desperate to escape (I can't help but think of an angry child locked against his or her will in the punishment closet). A television in the curator's quarters was found laying face down on the floor where it had mysteriously dropped three feet from where it was sitting. And just as strangely, it was still in perfect working order, as if it had been gently lowered there.

Many of the staff at the museum have had personal experiences with whatever shares the home with them, and they keep well-documented files and notes on each occurrence. But I think no staff member has had as terrifying a time as Lisa Higbee herself, the same curator who was reluctant to allow Dr. Greco to come and possibly "stir things up." She relates the following incident:

> Do you believe in ghosts? I'm not for sure that I do, but I do know that I once lived in a haunted house. Oh, I had heard stories of the house, but I didn't really believe them, not, at least, until I had to move into the house.
>
> It was pretty much like any other Victorian house. It had large rooms, somewhat overpowering, ornate and stuffy. But it was different from most in at least three ways. First, it had a cantilevered staircase that began on the first floor and wound around all the way up to the third floor. Second, the third floor was different . . . very dark from years of coal dust accumulation. Coal was burned to heat the house, the dust filtered to the third floor, where it was trapped and proceeded to become part of the walls, ceilings, floors—everything was all discolored and blackened like a moonless night. As you touched the walls you could feel the age-old grime soiling your fingertips. The third thing about the house deals with another darkness. Something indescribable, just a feeling. Something not quite right, a chill . . . a smell . .. a noise—something not quite right.
>
> But haunted? Humph!

For me, it all started with some lost keys. The keys to the servant's bedroom on the third floor. I went to the closet where they should have been, but they were missing. Upon inquiring of the people in the house. I learned that no one had seen them, nor could anyone remember the last time they had been to the locked room. It made no sense, there was no reason for any of us to mislead the other. But the keys were definitely missing. Later, as I entered one of the bedrooms, for some reason, I don't know why, I was drawn to the vanity and a vase on top. As the vase was lifted there was a slight jingle. Upon looking inside the vase I discovered the missing keys. Confronting the others with what I thought to be an apparently good, although misguided, hoax, they assured me that not one of them had hidden the keys.

We joked, "It must have been the ghost. Ooooo, hoooo, oooo, uuu, hoo." We started to talk about the ghost and the other unusual, inexplicable, occurrences in the house. We made fun of the ghost. We even gave "it" a name—"Cornelia"— after one of Mr. Culbertson's wives. We sometimes called her "Corny" for short.

"Corny, did you take the keys? Did you hide them? Did you lead me to the vase to find them? Are you here? Are we playing a game? Corny?" We made fun of the ghost. It wasn't a wise thing to do.

Several days later, we were all working together on an exhausting, yet exhilarating project. Relaxing for a moment, we lackadaisically relished in the silence. It was then that we heard the footsteps . . . overhead . . . from the third floor. But, how could that be? There was no one else in the house—or was there? Looking one from another, the perplexed glances confirmed that we all had definitely heard the noise.

It was decided that the footsteps needed to be investigated. I carelessly volunteered to go to the area from which they came. As I started up the stairs to the blackened third floor, Joellen whispered to me,

"Don't go alone, never go there alone." So we ventured together on towards the unknown that awaited us. Was there a chill? I could feel the grime from the walls, the darkness was more than on the surface. Halting at the top of the stairs, we caught one another's expression of foolish courage.

Together we started to check the rooms, nothing seemed out of order. As we entered the hallway, going to the other side of the house we heard a sudden "slam," the door behind us had to be forcibly shut. But, no. It was just as we left it. No, we heard that door slam, didn't we? Just as we had heard the footsteps . . .? I hurried to the other rooms, if there was someone here, I was going to catch them in the act! Nothing. No one. Lost in bewildered thought I walked back to the hallway.

"Jo, let's go. Jo?"

My friend was standing in the center of the hall, head bowed, arms in the victory pose; her body swayed and she was mumbling.

"Jo, are you all right? What are you saying?" I whispered.

In a vacant tone, she spoke: "Prince of Darkness, we rebuke you in the name of the Lord. You have no power here. Jesus Christ is the Savior of our lives. Prince of Darkness, begone in the name of the Son of God."

I thought that she had gone crazy. Maybe we had been working too hard. Then she turned to me and said, "Lisa, memorize these words. You might need them some day." I knew she had been working too hard. I didn't memorize the words, they seemed foolish and irrelevant. This could all be explained.

Things started to get worse several months later. That's when the dreams began. Minerva. Have you ever had a dream when you didn't know if it was really a dream or if it was real? You wake up wondering if the events happened, if your worries are true. Confusion overpowers logic.

The day was one of those dismal times and energy-sapping days. The rain was unceasing, the leaves were moldering in the gutters, all seemed dormant and in a state of decay. The house had a chill that wouldn't shake off. It smelled musty too. We were all in a mood befitting the environment. When evening came, it was welcomed as signaling the end of the day. A good night's sleep was well in order, an anticipated comfort. Was I wrong!

It was late in the night when the dream began. I could see myself arising from the bed, out of my room and going across the master bedroom, heading towards the third floor. In my mind I could hear the warning, "never go there alone," but I was unable to stop the sequence of events.

I wouldn't . . . I can't be doing this?!! As I climbed the stairs to the third floor, I knew that I was not alone. There was something. . . someone . . . Hesitantly, I looked over my left shoulder and there she was. A young girl, standing on the handrail of that cantilevered staircase. She was slight in build, wan, seeming pure, yet full of sorrow.

"Get down from there, honey, you'll fall."

"I know."

"Please get down . . . Who are you?"

"My name is Minerva," she breathlessly whispered.

What an odd name, I thought. "Mine's Lisa."

"I know."

"Well, Minerva, please don't stand on the handrail, I'm afraid you'll fall." It irritated me that she wouldn't move, just hovered over me on the handrail, swaying with careless abandon.

"All right," I resigned myself to her show of indolence, "So what are you doing here anyway?" Minerva proceeded to tell me her story, how her parents had died in a terrible accident and how she had been taken to the Children's Home, then selected by the family to live with them as a servant. She spoke of the family as I couldn't have known. Her life, her heart was filled with mournfulness. She told me how unhappy she was, how the family fought with one another. Vile, nasty emotions enveloped the house. There was much contempt, menace, and hatred. Minerva wished for death. I, without conviction, tried to persuade her that death was no answer. But she was unyielding.

"But, Minerva, what are you doing here now?"

"I was lonely, I called you and you came. We are going to be the best of friends."

"No, Minerva, I don't want to be any part of this. You see, I'm really not here—this is a dream. I can't be your friend, you don't exist. I'm going to wake up now and you'll be gone." She looked at me and the rejection tugged at my very being, then a smug grin overtook her pitiful features.

"I'll be back, and so will you."

With those words, my fear became a reality as she faltered and fell towards the stairs. It was all in slow motion, leaning over the stairs, I could see her falling . . . reaching, unable to yell, unable to help. Her little body turned over and I could see a contorted scream on her face, but no sound was uttered. All I could hear was "I'll be back, and so will you."

As she hit the first floor, I jerked up from my bed. Hardly able to breath, I listened through the silence. The thoughts of the nightmare consumed my waking moments. But, then they started, shattering the silence . . .the footsteps. "No, this is a dream, this isn't happening; it's all part of the dream." But the footsteps continued. You could follow their progress, on the third floor, from the hall, across the bedroom, towards the stairs. At the foot of the stairs was my bedroom. The footsteps were progressively getting closer. "No! Stop! I'm frightened."

I began whispering, "It's a dream, it's a dream, it's a dream, it's a dream, this is not happening."

The footsteps came increasingly nearer, louder, more distinct. "What was that prayer Jo told me to memorize?" I couldn't think, what once seemed fool-

ish now seemed vital. I tried other prayers, what were the words? Panic was taking over.

Unexpectedly, a calm overcame me as I realized that as long as I tried to face this as a dream, that I could not master it. It had to be a reality, it was a reality. The footsteps were outside my door, when the words came to me. Kneeling, I spoke with a new found conviction and courage,

"Prince of Darkness, I rebuke you in the name of the Lord. Jesus Christ is the Savior of my life. Prince of Darkness, you have no power here, begone. The Son of God rules over Darkness."

The footsteps stopped. There was a silence again. Collapsing in my bed, I must have fallen asleep. When I awoke the next morning, I was weary and felt like I had been beat. The others sensed my foul mood. Finally, Jo asked what my problem was. The story of the dream of Minerva clearly unfolded, the details were distinct . . . the uncertainty of its reality. When I was finished, I looked up and saw that my friend was pale, as she lifted her head from her hands, I could see that she had been crying.

"Jo, what's wrong?"

"You don't remember," she wept.

"But, I did remember, near the end, I remembered the words, your prayer, it saved me."

"No, you don't remember her name. Mrs. Culbertson."

"No," Jo continued as a mutual fear filled the room. "It was Cornelia Minerva Culbertson. Her name was Minerva."

The word "Minerva" echoed in my mind, secretly I knew that we'd meet again.

I don't know if you believe in ghosts, but even *I'm* still not sure that I do.

Incidents continue to this day to plague the staff of the Culbertson Mansion State Historic Site. A medium-sized harp sitting in the formal parlor keeps turning itself around. Now mind you, the harp is quite heavy, and has a detachable base. So not only is the harp found from time to time facing the wrong

The harp that moves by itself. Note the shadow in the upper left corner—the harp mover him/herself?

way, but so is the base, as if two men had moved it. Yet no one is around when the harp is found disturbed.

Last year, the staff of the mansion held a fund raising raffle, with the prize being a stay for the night in the house. Many entered, and there were a handful of winners. But even some of those who won turned down the prize, not wanting to even stay one night with whatever walks the hallways. Yet a few did stay. After a late dinner, all guests retired to their respective rooms, and the staff were locking up for the evening when suddenly they heard footsteps, lots of footsteps. They ran upstairs as the footsteps faded away, but found all the guests safely ensconced in their rooms. Probably just Cornelia checking up on her overnight visitors.

In March of 1996, Chuck and Jessica, both historic interpreters at the museum, had to go to the third floor to retrieve some objects from storage. Chuck opened the storage door, and entered the room, but stopped dead in his tracks. In front of him, a large spinning wheel was merrily turning away, rotating around and around. Chuck reached out his hand and stopped the wheel, which then remained motionless.

He breathlessly asked Jessica if she had seen what he had seen, but unfortunately, Chuck had blocked her line of vision, and she had seen nothing. Chuck left the room quite puzzled, not just from the spinning itself, but from the fact that the spinning wheel is quite stiff and not easy to turn. It would have taken quite a lot of force to set it in motion. No mere wind or draft could ever have done it.

On April 14, 1996, Dr. J. B. Haile and his family visited the mansion for the first time. They were not from New Albany, and had never heard of the Culbertson house before, or of its ghosts, and had decided on a whim to stop and take the tour. But something else went on the tour with them. He and the family were on the second floor in the middle of their tour. Dr. Haile had wandered over to the guest bedroom and was glancing down at the floor examining the detailed woodwork, when he caught sight of a woman in a dark grey skirt, complete with bustle, coming his way. She was wearing black boots, and passed him very quickly. He only glimpsed her from the waist down, as he did not have time to raise his head for a good look. And by the time he turned around, she was gone.

Immediately thereafter, Charlotte, a maintenance person and tour guide, heard footsteps in a different part of the second floor as if whatever had passed by Dr. Haile was continuing to walk ahead of them, as if to prepare the way.

I visited the Culbertson Mansion in early July, 1996. It was a typical midwestern July day, with moisture hanging in the air so thick you felt you had to swim to the front door. The place bulked larger than life as we, my photographer and I, approached on foot after parking some distance away. Heat lighting shimmered in the distance with the threat of an afternoon thunderstorm.

The Mansion looks like a cheery place from outside. It's brightly painted yellow walls seemed to beam in the muggy air. The place is full of surprises, and if you don't spend some time just looking about, you're liable to miss quite a bit. Such a case is the covered entry way. At first glance it's merely an enclosed porch, handy for escaping from the rain. But look up, and you're treated to a beautiful mural spreading out across the ceiling. Birds of bright colors mix with intertwining vines to give the illusion of blue sky above. Those are the kind of details that make the visit so rewarding.

Not surprisingly, the house has no air conditioning, so it is quite warm throughout the rooms. I had called ahead to warn them I was coming, and was greeted by Greg Worman, a historic interpreter for the museum. He took us on a fabulous tour of the home and filled us with details from the Culbertsons lives that brought the old house to life. Each room is a masterpiece, and just when you think you've been amazed enough, just turn the corner and be prepared to hold your breath. Inlaid woodwork, hand painted panels, vast gold leaf ceilings and all the trimmings of a bygone era made us both expect to see Mrs. Culbertson coming down the stairs to welcome us to her home.

The elegantly decorated rooms glinted in the soft light of turn-of-the-century lamps and late afternoon haze. To say that we were amazed is an understatement. The beauty of the house is not something that can be adequately put into words. It must be experienced. With the exception of the formal dining room, as it was under a complete renovation, Greg gave us the run of the house, pointing out details here, adding anecdotes there.

The cantilevered staircase, a truly massive affair carved from rosewood, climbs three stories up to the ballroom, and one can look up and see blue and red light softly filtering through a third floor stained glass window. I could very well imagine Cornelia peering over the rail, curious to see who came to visit today. As Greg, Chris, my photographer and I climbed to the third floor and rounded the last bend at the top of the stairs, a strange dizzy sensation came over us. We saw no grey lady, felt no icy winds nor the spectral touch of an unseen hand. We heard no footsteps. Yet we couldn't help but feel that someone was still there watching over the house that was their pride and joy.

And the ghostly happenings still go on. Perhaps Cornelia is pleased with the renovation work, and delights in leading visitors and staff through her wedding-present home, pointing out choice bits of work here and there. Perhaps the lingering traces of death, sickness, and overly-strict discipline taint the air in the grand structure. Or perhaps, just as simply, the Culbertsons are a little tired of visitors traipsing through their property and are simply looking for a bit of a respite. If you go there, maybe you can ask Minerva. I hear she's still searching for a playmate.

CHAPTER ELEVEN

A MORBID MISCELLANY
Spirits and Spooks too Unique to Classify

There are always those few stories that are impossible to categorize. This grisly grimoire of phantasms and specters simply defy definition . . .

The Unknown Corpse

In 1927, in the town of Peru, the government seat of Miami County, a disturbing discovery was made. Down in the depths of Jacob Rife's gravel pit, which sat about two hundred feet south of the banks of the Wabash River (right where today's west city park stands) something grisly came to light. While stripping gravel, workers came upon the skeleton of some poor human. The bones were buried in a sitting position, unceremoniously dumped into the hole of a crude grave about twenty-eight inches deep, with its head pushed down between its knees. No other item was found in the grave. No clothing. No jewelry. No scrap of information that might yield the identity of the poor soul.

Examination of the body at that time revealed that the victim was a man, probably of French nationality due to specific skull features. The hapless individual was past his middle years based on wear to the teeth, and the skeleton had apparently been buried for many years, as it was quite heavy from all of the mineral deposits washed into the bones by the action of the river. Naturally during the investigation, the oldest residents of Peru were asked if they remembered anything from their youth, any stories or tall tales that might help with the identification. No one did. Likewise, those interviewed swore there was never a cemetery anywhere near the Rife gravel pit. The investigators finally concluded that more than likely, the

The Wabash River in Peru where the skeleton of a man was found.

skeleton was the remains of a tragedy from the early Wabash River days, a dangerous and notorious time to be about on the waterway. After closing the books on the case, the bones were later presented to the Miami County Historical Society, where they were preserved for the Miami County Museum, and remain to this day in their collection.

After the discovery of the skeleton, residents reported seeing strange lights floating just above the ground near the gravel pit. Mournful cries floated on the night air and translucent mists crept about the trees. To this day, rumors persist that the spirit of the murdered soul lurks near the old gravel pit, seeking justice, and imploring any who come near on dark nights to help him dig his way out of his shallow grave. Or perhaps, rather then help on those dark and chilly nights, he is seeking company in his sandy abode.[45]

The Cable Line Ghost

The night was moonless, one of those late fall evenings made even more dank by the cold mist that hugged the ground. The car was traveling much too fast down Cable Line Road near Elkhart for even the best of driving conditions. Suddenly, as the eastbound auto approached the intersection of County Road 11, the hapless driver found he no longer had control of his machine. Time inside the car seemed to slow down. The driver knew it was over, knew he was going to crash, yet he fought desperately to right his car. But it was a case of too little too late. Perhaps he saw the large tree just before the impact, but he was going so fast, more than likely he didn't. The car plowed into the tree with a terrible impact. The driver was thrown through the windshield and into the tree. After the cleanup of the wreckage, people commented that they could see the very spot where the man had hit the tree. But curiously, the body of the victim was never found. Some say he miraculously walked away, or perhaps wandered in shock off into the woods, there to die from his injuries. But others have a different theory. They say the force of the impact was so great that the tree itself actually captured the man's body, and with it his spirit.

Each Halloween night since the awful crash the spirit tries to release itself from the trunk of the tree, though after all these years it has never succeeded. If you look closely at the tree as you drive west on Cable Line Road, perhaps you can make out the outline of the point where the man's spirit entered the tree, and where it remains today. But drive ever so cautiously.[46]

The Headless Riverman

Located in southern Harrison County two miles west of Mauckport is Haunted Hollow, a place with a story attached to it that will make your blood run cold. It seems back in the early 1800s river pirates used the caves and rock overhangs in that section of Indiana as a base of operations and a place of hiding when they were pursued by the authorities. They would wait in hiding in some secluded spot for a flatboat carrying unsuspecting travelers to come into view. Then they would rush from their place of concealment and attack the startled voyagers.

This attack by the river pirates was usually swift and sure. The people in the boats were either killed or taken as hostages, and their possessions were then divided between the river bandits. There were many such places along all the major rivers of commerce in the country in that time and Haunted Hollow was such a place.

During the early 1800s, a flatboat reached the ambush spot of the river pirates late one evening. Unaware that the criminals were lurking in the vicinity, the travelers tied up to the shore to spend the night. They lit a cozy little campfire on the back and had a pleasant dinner. One can imagine the aroma of coffee and skillet fried ham drifting through the dark trees that moonless night. After a full meal and a long day, the boatmen retired to their sleeping ticks back on deck to settle down for some much needed rest. Well, it did not take the cutthroats long to become aware of the boat's presence. They saw the fire's embers, smelled the food, and stealthily they crept up to the unsuspecting flatboat.

For some reason, one of the boatmen had decided to sleep on shore. A pirate, unaware of his presence, stumbled across his prostrate form in the dark. The startled boatmen yelled out in surprise and the alarm was given. The remaining boatmen pushed off into the river with great haste, leaving their comrade stranded in the midst of murderers.

Seeing their hoped for prize slipping from their grasp, the pirates were enraged. The unfortunate boatman who had been left behind alone had to face the wrath of the furious pirates. Unfortunately for the boatman that the pirates were not long in exacting their revenge. The boatman was shot and stabbed repeatedly and his head was cut off and thrown into the Ohio. The body of the riverman was left on the river bank for animals to ravish. This much we know as fact.

It was not many years later that settlers began to move into the Haunted Hollow area, forcing the pirates to push on in search of greener pastures. The reminder of their terrible history remained however. Soon the settlers began to report an apparition that had been seen roaming the river banks and the deep hollows that extended back into the surrounding hillsides.

The settlers were terrified. They reported that the phantom was headless and slowly stumbled along as if looking for something. Of course, the name Haunted Hollow was given to the ravine and it naturally became a place to avoid. The ghost was supposedly seen for years by many different people. Even today on dark nights some local residents claim this unearthly specter still prowls the hollow looking for its head, and for passage down the river.[47]

Waltzing Matilda

The Preston House is the oldest existing house in Terra Haute. It was built by George Dewees, a transplant from New Orleans, who wanted to show the Wabash Valley he was a man of wealth to be reckoned with. Dewees built his home in the manner of the mansions of the Old South, making it one of only a very few of its type ever built in Indiana. And even though the house may not look like much now, at one time it was a stately mansion.

Dewees was active in local affairs but was still not liked by the townspeople of Terra Haute, who considered him a nasty man with a violent temper. It was a well-known fact that Dewees had been involved in numerous duels, fights, and lawsuits in his lifetime. When he died in 1834, no mention was made of his wife Matilda who hadn't been seen in several years. While there was some speculation that she had left him due to his violent nature, most people believed she was the victim of his evil ways. As Dewees was a possessive man, viewing a wife as property rather than partner, his wife's decision to leave would have sent him over the edge. The talk around town of his abandonment by Matilda was more than he could stand. All the heads turning and whispering in gossip and mocking laughter finally pushed him past the point of no return, into the realm of murder.

Dewees knew what it was like to kill. He had shot a man in the back during a duel in New Orleans. That particular indiscretion cost him $50.00 and a week in jail. But killing your wife . . . that was another thing.

The legends say that after he had killed her there in the house, he bricked up her body in the fireplace in the east room. The key to this assumption seems to lie in the fireplace's appearance itself. In the west room, there are cupboards on both sides of the fireplace. But for some reason, the east room only has cupboards on one side only, the other side being bricked over.

Does Matilda's ghost haunt the house? Some say they have felt a ghostly presence while other have seen a misty light that passes through the hallways. But one of the more interesting observations came when the Vigo Preservation Alliance conducted a tour through the home in 1985. A psychic, who knew nothing of the home's past, felt a disturbance in the room said to be the last resting place of Matilda. She felt a mysterious force filled with wonder, frustration, and awe . . . it couldn't understand what so many people were doing in her home.

Dewees was also said to have been a slave trader, so he would most certainly have been angry over what came in the future for his home. The house became a station on the Underground Railroad, a resting place for fugitive slaves on their way to the freedom of Canada. But for some of those slaves, the Preston House became their final resting place.

One particular group of men, women and children, were spending the day underground, in tunnels designed to keep them safe from the local police who were duty bound to send them back to captivity thanks to the Supreme Court's Dred Scott decision. The slaves were safe from prying eyes, but nevertheless disaster struck. For some mysterious reason, the tunnel, which had been used many times as it was considered quite safe, collapsed, thus cutting off the air the slaves needed to breath.

The abolitionists on the surface knew what had happened, but a rescue was out of the question. What would happen if somebody snooping around were to call the authorities. After all, what would reasonably sane people be doing digging up a back yard in the middle of the night? If authorities found out the secret of the Underground Railroad, how many others would lose their chance for freedom? The decision was made, for the good of the greater numbers, that those trapped below would have to die, so close to freedom, and yet so far away.

Even today, in the still of a summer night, if you listen closely, you might still hear hymns, telling of a better day . . . right around the corner.[48]

The Odon Fires

Back in the 1940s, William Hackler and his family, a respectable middle class family living in the country near Odon, experienced something quite extraordinary. After Mrs. Hackler had served breakfast to her family one morning, she noticed the faint smell of smoke drifting down from upstairs. The family immediately set off to investigate.

They found the smoke coming from beneath a second floor bedroom window, and the wall was hot! As they pulled back the wallboard and plaster, they discovered the fire was coming from *inside* the walls. The fire department was called immediately and they had no problem subduing the blaze. But finding the cause of the fire was another matter. The house was not wired for electricity or was any other source of the combustion able to be identified. The Odon Fire Department was baffled.

The firemen packed up their gear, and proceeded back to the fire house. But no sooner had they left, another fire started inside a feather mattress. Shortly thereafter, from 8:00 until 11:00 a.m., no fewer than nine separate fires broke out all over the house.

Mrs. Hackler found a mattress in a different bedroom burning from the inside out. One fire fighter found a book, sitting on a small table where the reader had left it, burning from the inside out as well. A pair of Mr. Hackler's coveralls burst into flame and turned to ash. A wall calendar in the kitchen vanished in a flash of fire. Small objects all over the house continued to spontaneously catch fire during the morning. Finally, when all was said and done, there had been a grand total of twenty-eight separate fires within the Hackler home that day.

Rather than risk his family, Mr. Hackler ordered the mattresses be brought outside and the entire family slept beneath the open sky that night. He swore neither he nor his family would spend one more day in the house. He completely dismantled the house room by room, and with the salvaged lumber, rebuilt a new house a few miles away. Luckily, the Hacklers never had any other problems with their new home.

As an interesting side note, the family and their home were the subjects of a 1941 advertizing campaign launched by Traveler's Insurance Company in Colliers Magazine. The company used the Hacklers and their strange home as proof that you, too, would be covered by their fire insurance, no matter what kind of fire it may be . . . even spectral.[49]

The Shaking Cabinet

Sometimes its not so much a house that seems to be haunted, but rather an object. Many a modern-day psychic lay claim to the ability to sense vibrations, or emanations from particular items: a beloved bit of jewelry, or a much favored chair. I know of a majestic Steinway grand piano that to this day is watched over by its long-deceased owner, to whom it was her pride and joy. She is a peaceful, loving presence, never threatening. Yet ever does she watch over her dear instrument.

This incident comes from Kira*, a young woman who's parents live in the Southport area of Indianapolis. She has tried in vain to find a reasonable explanation for this event, but is still puzzled to this day.

"I was sitting in the family room at my parents' house a year or so ago", she told me. "My mom had gotten up and had gone into the bathroom. Dad and I were sitting quietly in the family room, he in a recliner, me on the couch, with the television on pretty low. They have one cat, and he was sitting curled up on a throw rug between us and the kitchen doorway, perfectly within our line of sight.

"For some reason, I found myself sort of watching him, as if knowing something was about to happen. Suddenly, his ears pricked right up, his eyes flashed open wide, and he jumped to all fours as if struck by a lightening bolt. He spun around and around, as if chasing something in the air, and suddenly came to an abrupt stop, the throw rug bunched up beneath his feet, staring right at an antique cherry china cabinet my parents have in the dining room, which is situated just off the family room."

Kira didn't think much of it at first. Definitely strange, but wrote it off as just that old cat doing weird cat things. She was just going to settle back into the program she and her father were watching, when suddenly the china cabinet started shaking. "First I heard it," she told me, "a low clatter, and then it started to get really loud. You could see the darn thing vibrating all over the place."

By this time her father had noticed the commotion, but he couldn't make any more of it than Kira. A couple of figurines fell off the top, and the cabinet rocked so much that it banged up against the wall over and over. The wall behind it is almost four inches away from the cabinet, and it didn't hit hard enough to do any real plaster damage. But it did hit it hard enough to knock down a pair of framed photographs that were hanging almost two feet away from the cabinet on the same wall. And as abruptly as the whole incident had started, it instantly stopped and everything became deathly silent. Kira estimates that the entire episode lasted maybe only five or seven seconds.

"I thought what the heck?!?!" she added, shivering just a bit as she retold the story. "I jumped up and ran over there, looking for anything that might have caused the racket. I picked up the things that had fallen off the top of the cabinet and off the wall, and tried to think logically about what had just happened. I figured something had fallen upstairs or in the basement and just shook the floor. But my father and I looked all over every room in the house, and everything was fine, nothing had fallen. And to make matters even more strange, I hadn't even felt the floor shake."

"The wall behind the cabinet is an outside wall, and I thought that maybe someone had hit the wall from outside. The grass was wet, so footprints would have been readily visible. But of course, there were none." Maybe air in a pipe in the wall or something along those lines, she wondered, but there are no pipes in that wall.

Kira decided to do an experiment. She grabbed hold of the cabinet with both hands and tried to shake it, just to see how much force it would have taken to make it rock the way she had just seen.

"Now this is not a small piece of furniture," she added. "It's about seven feet tall, two and a half feet deep, and six feet wide. It's made of solid cherry, and filled with plates, silver, glasses and other stuff."

Well, it took quite a lot of pushing on her part to push it back up against the wall where it began, let alone shake it rapidly back and forth. Whatever had shaken that cabinet around, and had been spotted by her parents' cat, it must have had a good amount of force behind it.

Kira has never been quite at ease in the house since then. "I don't feel anything there. I just don't ever want to see something like that happen ever again!"

The Angry Apartment

Vincennes has its share of haunts, more so than just about any Indiana town I've investigated. I've met and spoken to many people who have experienced strange and mysterious events in and around the town. One such person, Saundra Jessee, had an encounter there while a student that she is not soon to forget.

Saundra had a close friend, Terry*, who rented a small house. Like so many college rentals, it was nothing spectacular, but it had character, just the kind of place a college student could feel at home in. Terry thought he had found a real gem of a house. What he didn't know was that the father of the current owner had died suddenly in the house. His body was left undiscovered for several weeks. And to make matters worse, the poor man's dogs starved to death for lack of care after his untimely demise. And something, be it former owner or hungry dog, was sharing Terry's space without paying rent.

Terry moved in, and was quite comfortable, except for the voices he kept hearing. A deep male voice would taunt him incessantly, saying such things as "Stop pissing in my shower!" And while Terry was being chastised by the unseen man, a woman would begin to scold the man who was doing the chastising. These arguments would go on for hours, and they started to take a toll on Terry.

Other things in the house were not quite right. Light bulbs, freshly replaced, would burn out in a matter of hours. Newly-fixed appliances would break down again in a day. Objects Terry put down would vanish and reappear in other rooms. For example, Saundra went to visit Terry for an evening of late night studying. She set her notebook down on the arm of the couch, and went to the kitchen to get herself a soda. But when she returned, the notebook was gone. She and Terry searched high and low, but to no avail. Until they looked in the bathroom. Tucked under the sink, in a closed vanity, was Saundra's notebook.

And if all this was not enough, it was impossible to heat the small house. No matter what temperature the thermostat was set on, the house remained a steady sixty degrees. Terry had the both the furnace and thermostat checked for reliability, but the repairman found nothing wrong. The house remained cold. Terry tried everything to warm the place up, but new electric space heaters would burn out in a week, and electric blankets would develop mysterious shorts that, while not dangerous, would prevent them from working.

Finally Terry had had enough. He was not an irrational man, and could not simply accept that unseen forces were tampering with his abode. So in a vain effort to stop the occurrences, he checked himself into the mental disorders unit of the local hospital, convinced that he was imagining it all. The hospital ran every test they could think of, and found no illness, either physical or mental. So they sent Terry home.

He was not keen on the idea of living there by himself, so he asked Saundra to move in for a while, in the hopes that she could get to the bottom of what was going on. She was there for about three weeks when she too started hearing the voices. She heard somewhere faint yet near a man and woman arguing in hushed tones. She couldn't make out the words, but the tone was quite heated. As she would drift off to sleep, she would be jarred awake by the sound of dogs barking somewhere in the house. She tried to trace the sounds, but they seemed to radiate from all around, seeping out of the walls, echoing out of the plumbing pipes. The ghostly canines continued to bark up a storm, and she could hear them straining against their chains.

She had no answers for Terry. Not knowing what else to try, she conducted a "cleansing ritual," a ceremony where a person asks those who have died to leave, to move on into the next existence, past the veil that separates the living from the dead. She explained to the man and woman that they had indeed died, and that they needn't stick around any longer. She also encouraged the dogs to follow the people as they left. And from that point on, the disturbances quieted down, until they were practically nonexistent.

Terry remained in the house for the remained of the lease, but left shortly thereafter. Saundra has not been back to the house since her friend moved away, and she wonders, did the unseen tenants and their dogs sign a lease somewhere else as well?

The Leeper Home

Samuel Leeper bought a large tract of land on both sides of the St. James River. The old Navarre cabin stood on his land and he used it as a barn. The Leeper home was completed in 1888 and Samuel, his wife and three daughters (one of which is said to have had a very unhappy marriage) moved in. The Leepers lived in this home for many years until their death. The land across the river was then given to South Bend as a park to preserve it.

The next family to move into the Leeper home had no children. The husband was a hard worker and was rarely at home. His lonely wife was a fearful woman who was said to have experienced many unusual things in the house when she was there alone. She had hidden large hat pins and knives in every door frame and on every window ledge in the house. These were thought to be her protection should she need it. When this couple died, the house sat empty for several years until the current owners bought it.

By this time several other homes had been built near the Leeper house along North Shore Drive. After extensive remodeling, the family moved in. They were only there a few days when the woman was awakened in the night by the sound of a card table dropping on the floor in the front hall. She awakened her husband who investigated immediately. He found nothing out of place. Several weeks later he was home alone working when he heard a bedroom door slam. The windows and all outside doors were closed, so there was no reason for this door to slam.

This ghost is believed to be, perhaps, the unhappy daughter of Samuel Leeper seeking the happiness she knew before her unfortunate marriage. She still comes to visit the family, however she is much quieter now. The noise was just her way of welcoming the new family into her home. All the family still see her on rare occasions. She usually appears most often in early spring, and usually in the kitchen area. She appears as a loosely-defined shape of varying sizes. The shape is best defined as a white, gauzelike, poorly-shaped circle. Her visits are brief and always nonthreatening. The family seems to feel as though she were a comfortable part of their home. Perhaps she does experience there the happiness she was denied so long ago.[50]

The Celestial Note

Not so many years ago, Sam* was a student at Notre Dame, residing in Washington Hall. Only a small handful of students lived in the old building. They were a studious group and didn't get involved with a lot of the silly pranks of college-aged boys. The only time the hall rang with a lot of noise was a few days a week when the marching band practiced in the room downstairs. Sam was a trumpet player, so he enjoyed hearing the band practice, although his studies did not leave enough time for him to participate.

Late one night in November, while Sam was studying, and many of the hall residents were asleep, their quiet was shattered by a single long clear beautifully executed tone. Several of the students ran to Sam's room to yell at him for playing his trumpet in the middle of the night. He assured them that he didn't even have his trumpet there at school. When he finally convinced them that he didn't do it, they left. Several nights later they heard it again. This time they were sure that a band member was sneaking into the band room to play tricks on them. They took all the necessary steps to make sure that all the doors were locked securely at night.

The tone continued to sound, always a B flat and always just one note. It never came at the same hour, but it was always after midnight. They might go for several days without incident. Late one night, two of the students came to Sam's room to study. They seemed to seek each other's company late at night now. At about one thirty a.m., the note sounded clearly in the hall. Immediately after, they all heard a loud fluttering as if a bird were caught in Sam's room. They searched the room, but found nothing. Thereafter, each time they heard the tone, they always seemed to hear the fluttering sound close to their ears. The fluttering sound was experienced by each of them and they each always felt that it was something that was somehow in the room with them.

Sometime later, on a particularly quiet night, immediately following the blast of the horn and the fluttering sound, several doors slammed and footsteps could be heard running down the hall. They all dashed to the door, thinking they were about to get to the bottom of it all. But all they saw were other students, also poking their heads out of doors to catch the mysterious tone maker, each student with a makeshift club in his hand, ready to do battle with the unseen.

Once the footsteps were first heard, they continued on many a night. The doors that slammed were checked and always found to be securely locked. The footsteps became so regular that they could count them. The number was always the same as they ran down the hall and up the stairs.

Only one person in the hall had never heard the ghost. He was a great strong Irishman who worked hard all day and slept soundly all night. He often laughed and made fun of their fears. They decided to make sure he heard the ghost at least once.

One night they dropped some heavy weights on the floor of the room above his head. Then Sam blasted a B flat on a trumpet borrowed from the bandroom and another fellow slammed the door and ran down the hall. It worked! The Irishman ran yelling from the hall in the middle of the night. The next day he brought several priests in to rid their hall of the spirit. After that day, the spirit has never been heard from again.

Some of the speculation on who the ghostly resident of Washington Hall might have been has led to these possibilities:

1) George Gipper, a local man who slept on the steps outside the hall, and who, after contracting a sickness, died there soon after.
2) A steeple jack who was killed when he fell from a loft of the building during construction.
3) Brother Cajeton, who played a pickhorn and is thought to have died in the building.[51]

The Scratching at the Door

Not to be outdone by Notre Dame, Indiana University has its own ghostly tale from one of the residence halls. Three coeds were up late one evening in Reeve Hall doing some late night studying. They had stayed over semester break rather than go home in the hopes of catching up on assignments. When Clair*, who slept in a connecting room to the other students, went to get some food, the other two girls did not worry much when she did not return right away. As time passed, they assumed Clair had simply gone to bed. So without much thought to the matter, they themselves wrapped things up for the night and went to sleep.

The two girls awoke the next morning and dressed quickly to run some errands. They opened their door and turned to leave when they stopped dead in their tracks. Clair had never made it back to her room. They found the poor girl's body just outside her own door. Clair had been clawing at the door in a vain effort to make it inside from something unspeakable, her face a mirror of the last horrible thing she must have seen as she died. Many students claim still that Clair walks the halls, trying to get back to her room. And if you listen carefully late at night, you can hear faint scratches on the dorm room doors of Reeve Hall.[52]

Dillinger's Picnic

Many talk of the spectral gathering near Mooresville at the site of the old farm once owned by the father of John Dillinger. People say at a certain time of the day on May 22, phantom laughter and merriment is heard and some even claim to have witnessed a ghostly group apparently picnicking beneath the trees. There have also been reports of the distinct smell of fried chicken drifting on the spring breeze from this spot which has been uninhabited for many, many years.

It is interesting to note that it was on May 22, 1934, that John Dillinger visited his family at the farm, and relatives, neighbors, and the press were invited for a picnic lunch which included fried chicken, biscuits and gravy, vegetable dishes, and numerous pies and cakes.

Oddly, the occurrences of the spectral gathering seem to date only as far back as the mid to late seventies. Interestingly, a number of people do not believe that the man killed outside the Biograph Theatre on July 22, 1934, was actually John Dillinger. Jay Robert Nash, Chicago author and crime historian, obtained the autopsy report and discovered that the dad man had brown eyes—Dillinger's eyes were blue.

Lee Holloway, an Indiana historian, went so far as to contact the undertaking establishment that had handled the funeral. She had found so many Hoosiers that did not believe the Dillinger had been gunned down in 1934, she thought there might be some validity to it all. She was told unequivocally that the corpse had not been that of John Dillinger. In fact, Dillinger's own father, upon looking at the body the first time, remarked, "He has changed considerably." Could Dillinger have changes so much from the time of the picnic in June to the time of his supposed death in July that his own father would not recognize him?

Jay Nash alleges that the man killed was actually James "Jimmy" Lawrence, a small-time hoodlum who resembled Dillinger in some respects. Assuming the man killed was not

Dillinger, this might account for the phantom picnickers being relatively new apparitions. After all, it would be terribly bad manners if the revelers began their festivities until the actual John Dillinger had joined them on the other side.[53]

Into the Wild Blue Yonder

Would it be any wonder that a ghost might be prowling around a place of war, a place linked with the fear and uncertainty of the Cold War and the 1960s? Many places of conflict are said to be haunted. Take for example the numerous Civil War battle fields that are said to still be patrolled by infantryman, both Union and Confederate. There are said to be more reported ghosts than you can shake a stick at prowling around the flying machines of war preserved at the United States Air Force Museum at Wright Patterson Air Force Base in Dayton, Ohio. But you needn't drive to Virginia or Ohio to find these ghostly warriors. Indiana has its own.

Fifteen miles north of Kokomo, near the town of Bunker Hill, sits Grissom Air Reserve Base, a sole survivor of the might of the Hoosier war machine developed during the World War II era. Now drastically cut back and scaled down, sharing its runways with Air Force Reserve KC-135 tankers, Grissom was not always the way one sees it today. For many years, it was known as Bunker Hill Air Force Base, the home of the 305th Bomb Wing. For there at Grissom were stationed during the 1960s the mighty B-58 Hustlers, the country's premier supersonic nuclear attack bombers. These imposing demons of the nuclear age were stationed only at one other Air Force base, so Bunker Hill was strategically vital to the nation's defense.

With its long, triangular delta-shaped wings, narrow pinched body, four massive jet engines, and nuclear tactical pod slung beneath it, the Hustler looked for all the world like some giant deadly wasp, one capable of supersonic speeds and of killing millions with just one sting. These birds were so hot, so fast and so tricky to fly that mishaps were not uncommon both over the skies and on the ground at Bunker Hill. These bombers were so technically advanced that one mistake behind the controls would mean sure death. And for one pilot, it was a death he could not immediately walk away from.

Imagine for a second you're back in the days of Nikita Khruschev, the Cuban Missile Crisis, and school-time nuclear attack drills. The B-58s would practice their bombing runs (sometimes it's rumored with actual nuclear weapons) over the skies of north central Indiana. And when finished, would come on in at fantastic speeds to land on the runways of Bunker Hill. And while the planes were the responsibility of the pilot while airborne, once on the ground, they became the possession of the crew chief, a man assigned to one specific plane to oversee all maintenance and care of the deadly bird. One old crew chief, Bill*, told me the fate of his Hustler, and its pilot.

One cold winter's day in late 1968, a B-58, with a crew of three, was making its landing approach, coming in against the strong cross winds that still rip across the open fields. The pilot knew he was in trouble as his craft began to wobble in the currents and he brought the nose up to compensate. He touched down, the back wheels skidding on the pavement, and he released the drag chute, but something went wrong. The front landing gear collapsed, and the Hustler plowed down the runway on its belly, luckily without its nuclear pod beneath. Fires broke out in the cockpit as the plane lurched to a halt. The copilot and weapons officers blew the hatches over their heads and escaped down emergency egress ropes, running to safety. But the pilot was not so lucky. He was killed as flames engulfed the front of the cockpit. Fire crews worked desperately to save him, but to no avail.

Later that afternoon, after the fires had cooled, the bomber was towed through the deepening snow back to its hanger to await a post-crash inspection and final salvage. It was locked down, and the bulk of the base retired for the night. Tom wanted to make a final inspection of the craft, to make sure all was shut down, that there was no chance of any further fire

P. Reed

outbreaks. He left the hanger building and walked through the snow to the Hustler, lying cold and dark in the falling night. But Tom was not alone.

As he stood next to the hulk, he noticed fresh footprints leading away from the front of the aircraft, from where the pilot might have jumped to safety had he been able to. Maybe the footprints of another technician, thought Tom. But the only tracks leading to the plane were his own, and the snow was deep enough that it would have shown any others. He was about to write it off as the workings of grief and an overactive imagination, when he suddenly realized where the tracks were headed. They led away from the cockpit straight back to the Alert Facility, where the pilot would have gone for a mission debriefing immediately after his landing. With a strange chill down his back, Tom followed the tracks to just outside the Alert Facility, where they slowly faded out and vanished.

Tom stood there in the falling snow, not knowing what to think. Did he tell his commander, or his friends? He didn't think so. The Air Force, he thought, would not take kindly to ghost stories about its nuclear attack force. He simply wished his friend clear skies and no cross winds, and returned quickly to the hanger, very shaken by what he had seen.

If you drive by Bunker Hill, now called Grissom Air Reserve Base, you'll notice just outside the gate a collection of veteran war birds. The Grissom Air Museum stands as a tribute to all service men and women who have come and gone in the name of their country. Among the collection of aircraft stands a lone B-58 Hustler, one of only six left in the entire world. And although not the same bird that crashed that fateful day, it too caught on fire and burned. As you stand in its shadow, look up at the cockpit, at the smoke-blackened windows that seem to beckon you to join the lost pilot, who perhaps, as that famous poem "High Flight" so eloquently states, has reached out and touched the face of God.

The Strange Phenomena of the "Old Hag"

Old Hag attacks occur, or at least are reported more frequently, in settings that are considered "haunted." This may be a case of "Which comes first, the chicken or the egg?" Does a house with a reputation of being haunted encourage someone to interpret the experience as supernatural or does a genuine supernatural experience itself promote the house to be called haunted? In poring over collections of both contemporary and past ghost folklore from around the world, I noticed that Old Hag attacks accompany other manifestations with startling frequency. What is the Old Hag, you ask?

The "Old Hag" manifestation seems to be identical, no matter in which country it occurs. The occurrence begins more often than not with the victim asleep, or near sleep, drifting somewhere in that nether region that is neither conscious nor dreaming. Quite suddenly, the victim feels a tremendous cold dead weight lay down on top of them, as if someone had just crawled into bed and rolled on top of them. The helpless person feels unable to breath, unable to move, and unable to shake the weight from off of their chest.

In some occurrences, the victim actually sees an old ugly woman lying above, leering down at him or her. The victim continues to grow short of breath, and either passes out, or the phenomenon simply dissipates as quickly as it began.

These "attacks" have been reported for centuries across Europe and the Americas. The medieval church quickly classified the disturbances as succubi, women demons who sexually molested men during the night. But despite religious definitions, the attacks continue to this day. Be it demon, ghost or dregs from our collective unconscious, something strange is going on.

Our example begins with Denise*, who, in the late 1960s, was a 22-year-old Purdue college student. Denise had just moved into a large apartment in a rehabbed Victorian building in West Lafayette. Although there was a bit of an unnatural chill to the place, she just couldn't say no to the low rent. The stately old house had sat vacant for about twenty years following a fire, and the new owners were anxious to get the recently renovated rooms occupied. The apartment had hardwood floors, stained glass windows, and a front parlor with a circular turret complete with carved marble fireplace. Her three roommates and she drew lots for room assignments, with Denise getting the parlor, which seemed to be the choicest room in the house.

One night during her first week there, Denise went to bed in a fine mood. She had not been drinking and despite the times, she didn't do drugs. She turned out the light and settled down to go to sleep. But as she was lying in bed thinking about the previous day's classes, she became aware of a rustling sound emanating from the turret. She focused on the sound, trying to determine its origins. A breeze over papers? A mouse? But as soon as she had dismissed these possibilities, the rustling sound stopped and was replaced by the sound of stealthy shuffling footsteps that were headed in her direction. Suddenly, the sense of a presence was so intensely strong that it filled the room, leaving her terrified. She lay on her back, the covers pulled tightly over her head, terrified of what was coming her way, when the next thing she knew she was completely paralyzed, not able to move even a finger.

The footsteps continued their approach and then, when she felt she could not be any more frightened than she was, a tremendous weight settled down on her chest, forcing her into the mattress. She felt a menacing presence, a personality at work that wanted to meddle with her in particular. Something very nasty and very old! The intense dreadful weight continued to press down on her, almost like a large animal settling itself on her body, pushing her almost through the mattress. She knew she was awake, that she was not dreaming, and that something evil was in the room with her. In that instant, somehow, thoughts of her childhood years of Sunday School came into her mind and she prayed to be released. In that instant, it was over. The following morning, she tried to tell herself that it had been just a dream. To this day, twenty-five-odd years later, she is sure she was not dreaming.

After that terrible night, she religiously slept with the light on and her bedroom door open. Months later, one of her roommates, Anne*, was sick with the flu. The heating system never quite took the chill off Anne's bedroom, so Denise, not thinking anything of it, offered to switch with her until she felt better. That night, Anne stayed in Denise's room and closed the pocket doors. The rest of household was watching TV elsewhere in the mansion with a number of friends. Sometime after midnight, they all heard the doors of Denise's room screech open on their runners and slam into their recesses in the wall. Anne came screaming down the hall, saying that something had sat on the bed. She felt the bed sag beneath the weight, though in her case, it wasn't on top of her. She also felt and heard something clawing and scraping at the bedspread.

After Anne's experience, she and Denise decided to share a room and kept the hall light on. Nothing like those two nights ever happened again. They left that place at the end of the school year and found another old apartment that proved to be just fine. The students who moved into their former place reportedly had problems there, too. Unfortunately, Denise was never able to compare stories with them.

So where do all these tales of the unseen leave us? Are all to be believed verbatim, or are they simply contrivances of urban myth? But even more importantly, what do we do with these tales? Do we run for the nearest closet, there to dive in and cover our heads with the closest blanket, praying that what we just barely glimpsed was nothing more than a visual mirage? Or do we approach, with trepidation but with curiosity, determined to learn the truth behind that which fears us most? I vote for the latter. I believe that no matter how far science stretches our understanding of the world around us, it will always leave us with more questions than answers, more gaps in our knowledge than science can adequately fill. And strive as we might, there will always be those things that we simply do not understand.

So relax in the knowledge that answers aren't required. Only an open mind and the willingness to believe that something beyond our five senses may be living side by side with us is necessary to open the door to understanding. Who knows, maybe the next time you run into a ghost, you just may be tempted to go up and shake its hand.

APPENDIX
TIDBITS & TEASERS

The following snippets of the supernatural were either too incomplete to follow up on with any success, or were discovered too late for complete inclusion in the previous chapters. If any intrepid readers have any information regarding these little bits, or information on any other haunted sights, I would love to hear from you.

- The ghost of Mrs. Standfield, an early curator of the Northern Indiana Historical Society, who has kept the staff of the old 1855 courthouse museum company for years.

- Near Harris City, a ghostly farmer walking his prize bulls wanders the fields.

- A headless horseman gallops around the landscape where Johnson, Monroe, Lawrence, and Brown Counties converge.

- Near Utica, a band of ghostly Indians carry on a so-far-fruitless search for a lost silver mine.

- In Letts, a small baby is often seen crawling and moaning mournfully for its mother.

- A spectral old woman with a lantern carries on an eternal search for her lost husband who slipped out of a boat into the murky depths of Lake Weimer. Hundreds of Boy Scouts have been scared witless by the sight of her aimless meanderings as she floats just off the surface of the lake peering into the depths for her drowned love.

- In Leiter's Ford there is a feisty rocking chair that, having a mind of its own, never seems to stay put.

- Rochester has a ghost that came and went only to come back again. (I never learned what kind of ghost, unfortunately.)

- Again in Rochester, a woman has claimed over the years to hear a baby wailing within the walls of her home.

- And finally from Rochester, people yet see mysterious glowing orbs out on Olsen Road.

- The Purple Lady of Disko lives in local gravel pits and is a harbinger of doom.

- Travelers are said to have encountered a floating orb of light on a lonely road between Leesburg and North Webster. The sphere seems to be harmless, but it has been known to follow visitors for some distance, or at times, chase them from its domain.

- Mysterious sounds have been heard emanating from the basement of the public library in Warsaw on at least one occasion. Cries of distress occurred as staff members were closing one night. No explanation was ever found. As the library is located near a known underground railroad station, perhaps the spirits of freed slaves still inhabit the area.

- There was a ghost in the old West End School building. The building stood where the Billings School is today. It was completed in 1863 at the cost of $12,000 and it cost a man his life as he fell to his death during construction. His spirit refused to rest until the building was torn down. For many years, a form of punishment at the school was to send a wayward student alone into the basement, where the spirit of the fallen worker was said to reside.

- Charmayne Pigg of Peru has reported that her home is haunted by the ghost of Rebecca Wilkinson, wife of Ratcliff

Wilkinson, the original owner of her house. Rebecca is said to be dressed in black, carries a white handkerchief, and is always sobbing. Mrs. Pigg speculates that Rebecca is remorseful because after the death of her husband she sold the right-of-way across their land to the Denver, Eel River, and Indiana Railroad, whereas her husband had only agreed to lease it. Ratcliff Wilkinson (1810-1871) was one of the first settlers in Jefferson Township in Miami County having arrived there in the fall of 1830.

- A ghost train has been reported from time to time near Culver Station, seven miles southeast of Lafayette. Apparently, in 1864 there was a head-on crash of two trains that resulted in the deaths of thirty passengers, and the injury of thirty more. People have heard the roar of a passing train, felt a rush of wind and a trembling of earth, and then an ear-splitting crash followed by the moans of the dead and dying.

- Hannah House in West Central Indianapolis is allegedly haunted. Built by Alexander Hannah in 1858, it was supposedly a stop on the underground railroad. One tale tells of a lamp that tipped over, causing the death of several escaped slaves. Some people have reported the smell of rotting flesh coming from one of the upstairs bedrooms.

- A ghost is rumored to haunt the Murat Shrine Temple in Indianapolis.

- A spirit from a seance is said to haunt a house of a Morgan County man.

- The Dove's Nest, a notorious brothel located above a shop in old downtown Corydon in the 1800s, is reported to have many a spirit.

ENDNOTES

1. Bell, Steve; *Indianapolis Monthly*, October 1983.

2. *Indiana Rural News*, October 1975.

3. *Indiana Preservationist*, September-October 1989.

4. Baker, Ronald; <u>Hoosier Folk Legends.</u>

5. Ibid.

6. Ibid.

7. Ibid.

8. Jessee, Saundra; Usenet, Alt.folklore-ghost stories.

9. Ibid.

10. *Washington Press*, Salem, December 7, 1974.

11. Harp, William; *The Elkhart Truth*, October 1984.

12. <u>Kosciusko County History,</u> p 25, 1986.

13. *Harrison County Press*, Volume 104, Number 46, March 2, 1973.

14. Clements, William and Lightfoot, William, <u>Indiana Folklore,</u> Volume 5, 1972, p. 92-141.

15. Hanson, Larry L.; *Indiana Rural News*, October 1975, p 7.

16. <u>Haunted Road Trip,</u> Vigo County Historical Society.

17. Ibid.

18. Neff, Nancy; *The Sentinel*, Rochester, Indiana, October 31, 1989.

19. Hansen, October 1975, p 7.

20. Hartman, J. & Reznik, S.; The Spirit of South Bend, South Bend Community School Corporation, 1984.

21. Olsen, Steve; Usenet, Alt.folklore-ghost stories.

22. Haunted Road Trip, Vigo County Historical Society.

23. Kelsey, Julie; *Warsaw Times Union*.

24. Hanson; October 1975, p 7.

25. Holloway, Lee; Correspondences, 1984

26. Haunted Road Trip, Vigo County Historical Society.

27. Jessee, Saundra; Correspondences, 1995.

28. Hanson; October 1975, p 6.

29. Himebaugh, Eleanor; *Bedford Times-Mail*, October 31, 1983.

30. Himebaugh, October 31, 1985.

31. Himebaugh, October 31, 1984.

32. Denny, Dann; *Bloomington Herald-Telephone*, October 29, 1987.

33. Schaperjohn, Selma, editor; *Where There's a Willard*, 1985.

34. Kosciusko County History, p 25, 1986.

35. Hartman, J. & Reznik, S.; The Spirit of South Bend, South Bend Community School Corporation, 1984.

36. Kriebel, Robert; *Lafayette Journal and Courier*, June 24, 1979.

37. Morning Glory; *Lafayette Morning Journal*, August, 1890.

38. Hartman & Reznik; 1984.

39. Encyclopedia of Psychic Phenomena, 1983.

40. Jones, Chloeann; *Sentinel Correspondent*, October 27, 1987, p 2.

41. Willard, Shirley, editor; Fulton County Folks, Volume 2, 1981, Fulton County Historical Society, Rochester, Indiana.

42. Haunted Road Trip, Vigo County Historical Society.

43. Cotten, Tony; *The Weekly*, June 23, 1994, p 1.

44. Cotten; June 23, 1994, p 1.

45. Miami County Historical Society, 51 North Broadway, Peru, Indiana 46970.

46. Harp, October 29, 1984.

47. Allison, Harold; *Valley Advance*, January 9, 1979, p 16.

48. Haunted Road Trip, Vigo County Historical Society.

49. *Collier's Magazine*, April 19, 1941.

50. Hartman & Reznik; 1984.

51. Ibid.

52. Hanson, October 1975, p 7.

53. Holloway, Lee; correspondences.